The Companion Guide to
FamilyTree
Maker 2011

D1119558

The Companion Guide to
FamilyTree
Maker 2011

TANA L. PEDERSEN

ancestry publishing

Library of Congress Cataloging-in-Publication Data

Pedersen, Tana L., 1973-
 The companion guide to Family tree maker 2011 / Tana L. Pedersen.
   p. cm.
 Includes index.
 ISBN 978-1-59331-336-4
 1. Family tree maker. 2. Genealogy—Computer programs. 3. Genealogy—Data processing. I. Title.
 CS14.P426 2011
 929'.10285--dc22

                                           2010028544

Contents

Contents

Chapter 10   Running Reports 161

Introduction

Congratulations on selecting Family Tree Maker to discover and preserve your family's heritage. It's quick and easy to use for those just starting to research their family history, but it's also robust enough for the most serious genealogist. Use Family Tree Maker to store, display, and print any kind of family information you want—from names, birth dates, marriages, and deaths to priceless family stories, pictures, and audio/video files.

This guide is designed to help you learn Family Tree Maker 2011 quickly, leaving you more time to discover your family history. Even if you have never used a genealogy program before, you will find that the Family Tree Maker interface and options make it possible to keep track of even the most tangled of family trees.

This book is written with the novice computer user in mind. You will read about many of the useful features that the casual Family Tree Maker user never discovers, and you will be taken on a hands-on trip through the Family Tree Maker program. The many illustrations let you check your progress as you master each new feature or concept. Even if you are familiar with computers, though, you may have only recently been introduced to Family Tree Maker or simply want to know what great features you have not yet discovered in the program. This book offers you a step-by-step tour of the program and all that you can accomplish with it.

Before you begin entering your family's information, be sure to check out the "Family Tree Maker Basics" chapter. It will give you the basic skills you need to navigate through Family Tree Maker and will make you familiar with the software's interface.

What's New in 2011?

Family Tree Maker 2011 introduces more than 100 enhancements (including an updated look and feel!) to help you create your family story like never before. Here are just a few of the exciting new features you'll enjoy:

- **Smart Stories™—a narrative tool.** If you've always wanted help starting your own family history book, this is the tool you've been waiting for. Smart Stories helps you quickly fill up those blank pages by letting you use facts, sources, and notes you've already entered in your tree. Simply drag-and-drop the text into your story. And Smart Story text is linked to your tree so if you make changes, the text will be updated automatically.

- **New and improved charts.** In addition to four new fan charts, you'll be able to enhance your charts with new backgrounds, borders, and embellishments. You can even change fonts based on fact types.

- **New and improved reports.** Ancestor and descendant reports have been improved and added to. You'll also find a new Surname Report, the ability to sort custom reports, and the option to save and reuse report settings.

- **Better Ancestry integration.** Ancestry.com has millions of members all over the world. And now you can find out which members are searching for your ancestors by viewing Member Connect activity in the expanded Web Dashboard. You'll also see links to message boards and notification of your new Ancestry messages. In addition, uploading and downloading speeds have been improved. And once you've uploaded your tree, try out our free Ancestry iPhone® app, which lets you view and edit your online tree from your iPhone (available on iTunes).

- **New media management tools.** Now you can drag-and-drop, cut-and-paste, and even categorize multiple items at the same time. You'll also find a new tool that helps you locate missing media files.

How the Guide Is Organized

As you read this book, you'll notice several features that provide you with useful information:

- **Tips** offer you timely hints about features and additional ways of performing tasks.

- **Notes** give you guidance on the best ways to complete tasks.

- **Sidebars** give you additional information on a variety of family history topics, such as maps and media items, that will enhance your ability to create a richer and more complete family tree.

- A **glossary** explains terms you might not be familiar with, such as technical computer terms (icon, URL), Family Tree Maker terms (family group view, Fastfields), and genealogy terms (GEDCOM, Ahnentafel).

If you still need help, a quick perusal of the Table of Contents should lead you right to the task you are trying to perform; if not, check the index in the back of the book.

Part One

Getting Started

Chapter One
Installing Family Tree Maker

This chapter lists the system requirements for using the software, shows you how to install Family Tree Maker on your computer, and gives you a quick introduction on getting help as you're working in Family Tree Maker.

System Requirements

The computer equipment you will need is shown on the next page. Keep in mind that the more family information you enter, the greater the amount of free hard drive space and available RAM you will need. If you plan to include many images or videos in your trees, you will need a substantial amount of hard drive space.

If your system does not meet these minimum requirements, we cannot guarantee that the program will function correctly. You will need to upgrade your system to meet these requirements if you want to use Family Tree Maker 2011.

Installing Family Tree Maker

To use Family Tree Maker, it must be installed on your computer's hard drive. You cannot run it directly from the original CD. If you already have a version of Family Tree Maker installed on your hard drive, it will remain on your computer. The new one will not copy over the old one. While this installation process will not harm your existing Family Tree Maker files, it is always a good idea to keep a backup of your files in a different location such as on a flash drive, CD, or DVD.

Family Tree Maker utilizes an automated installation system—built into the CD-ROM—making setup fast and easy.

Recommended System Requirements

- Operating system: Microsoft Windows® 7/ Windows XP SP2/Vista™
- Processor: 1GHz Intel Pentium® III (or equivalent)
- Hard disk space: 460MB for installation
- Memory: 1GB RAM
- Display: 1024x768 resolution monitor
- 32X CD/CD-R (Required for installation. Some supplemental products require a DVD-ROM drive.)

All online features require Internet access. User is responsible for Internet Service Provider (ISP) account, all Internet access fees, and phone charges.

Minimum System Requirements

- Operating system: Microsoft Windows® XP SP2/Vista™
- Processor: 500MHz Intel Pentium® II (or equivalent)
- Hard disk space: 460MB for installation
- Memory: 512MB RAM
- Display: 800x600 resolution monitor
- 2X CD-ROM (required for installation)

Note: System configuration may require minor adjustments to the configurations of your operating system and/or updates to the hardware component drivers. As with all Windows programs, a faster processor, more RAM, and more free disk space enhances performance.

Insert the Family Tree Maker Installation Program CD into the CD drive. When the launcher appears click the **Begin Installation** button and follow the instructions on the screen; if the Setup Installer doesn't automatically launch, click the Windows **Start** button and then select **Computer**. Double-click the icon for your CD drive. Then follow the instructions on the screen.

- **Welcome**—The Setup Installer begins running automatically, displaying a series of screens welcoming you to the program and asking you to read and approve the license agreement.

- **Choosing Destination Location**—The normal destination directory for Family Tree Maker is a folder called Family Tree Maker 2011 located in the Program Files folder on your hard drive. In most instances, this will be your "C" drive.

- **Setup Status**—You will see messages and status bars as the appropriate files are installed on your hard drive.

- **Setup Complete**—After completing the installation process, click **Finish**.

Registering the Software

Before you create your first tree, take a minute to register the software. We offer registered users of Family Tree Maker the following special benefits: the powerful Family Tree Maker Web Search feature and the ability to merge Ancestry.com records into your tree; access to dynamic maps; discounts on future versions of Family Tree Maker; and notifications of updates.

From the **Help** menu, select **Register Family Tree Maker**. Then follow the instructions on the screen.

Activating an Ancestry.com Subscription

If you are already a member of Ancestry.com or if a trial membership came with your Family Tree Maker purchase, you can activate your subscription within the software. Once you've activated your account, you can use the Web Search feature to merge Ancestry.com records into your tree.

From the **Help** menu, select **Activate Ancestry Subscription**. Then follow the instructions on the screen.

Getting Help

Family Tree Maker has a built-in Help system and access to tutorials and an on-line technical support. If you have questions about a software feature or simply want to learn more about the program, check out one of these Help resources. And don't forget to check out the troubleshooting chapter in this guide.

Help Program

Family Tree Maker has a convenient, built-in Help program (fig. 1-1). At any time, you can access Help for the current window you are viewing or editing. You can also search the Help program by typing in a topic or phrase, then viewing and/or printing the resulting explanation.

Figure 1-1

The Welcome window in the Help program.

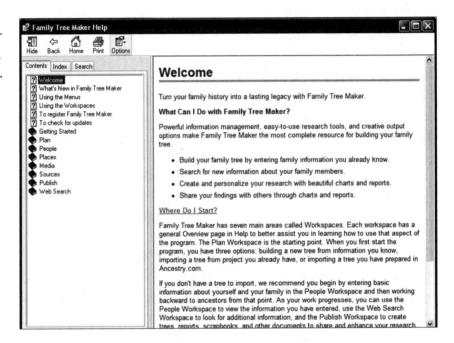

Accessing the Help Program

From the **Help** menu, select **Help for Family Tree Maker**; or press the **F1** key (located at the top of your keyboard) and click the **Show** button. Family Tree Maker displays the Help window:

- **Contents tab**—displays a list of Help topics arranged logically in chapters, like the table of contents of a book. Each chapter is identified by a book icon. You can double-click a book to see the contents of each chapter. For chapters with sub-chapters, double-click on the subsequent book icons (sub-chapters) until you funnel down to individual Help topics. Read individual Help topics by clicking on the topic you are interested in. The topic will be marked with a question mark in a square and will appear in the left panel of the dialog box.

- **Index tab**—works like a book index. Find the term you want and double-click it to see the corresponding Help topic.

- **Search tab**—lets you search for words or phrases that may be contained in a Help topic.

Searching in the Help Program

Click the **Search** tab and do one of the following:

- **Type the first few letters of the word you're looking for**—This field is where you enter the word, phrase, or topic you want to know more about. Many useful topic pages can be found by entering the keywords "adding," "creating," "displaying," "entering," "individual(s)," "information," and other action words.

- **Use the scroll bar to select the index entry you want**—Once the keyword or phrase you're looking for is highlighted, click **Display**.

The Help page opens. If there is more than one choice for your entry, Family Tree Maker may display a second window. Simply make your selection and click **Display** again.

Navigating in the Help Program

The built-in Help program makes extensive use of "links" to take you to other related topic pages. These links are easily identified by their blue, underlined text. Simply click on any link to go to a new topic page. Once there, you can click **Back** to return to the previous page or click the Index tab to return to the Index. Use these options to move around within the Help program:

- **Hide/Show**—Click to return to the tab view of the Help window or vice versa.

- **Back**—Click to move back through the series of Help pages you have navigated using the blue, underlined text links. When you get back to your original Help page, this option will be grayed out and unavailable.

- **Forward**—After using the Back button, click to move forward through the help items from which you backtracked.

- **Print**—Click to print the currently selected Help page. A print dialog box will be displayed from which you can select any available options, then print the page to keep for future reference.

- **Options button**—Click to display a sub-menu of additional options, such as "Search Highlight On," which you can use to highlight search terms on a Help page.

Tutorials

Family Tree Maker includes a variety of tutorials that illustrate and explain how to use Family Tree Maker (fig. 1-2). With these tutorials—available directly from your software—you will quickly learn how to organize, research, and share your family history.

Figure 1-2

A tutorial about the People workspace.

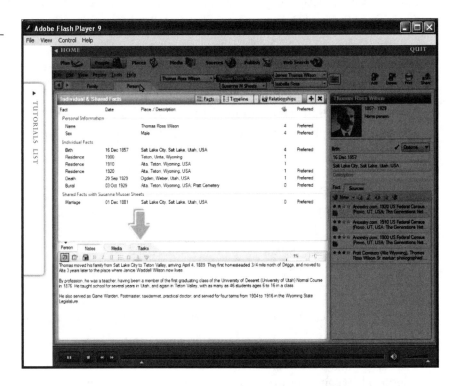

Ancestry.com Blog

The Ancestry.com blog <blogs.ancestry.com> contains the latest company news, information about searching for your ancestors, tips on using Family Tree Maker, and more. Want to know when the next webinar is? Interested in seeing which databases were just released? Check the blog. And don't forget to leave your own comments and questions.

1. From the **Help** menu, select **Training Tutorials**. The tutorial window opens. On the left side of the window, you'll see a list of topics you can choose from; each one correlates to a workspace in the software.

2. Click a topic to launch the tutorial.

Companion Guide

This *Companion Guide* can be viewed as a PDF on your computer. To access the guide, select **Companion Guide** from the **Help** menu. The guide will open. If you are not able to view the PDF, you may need to install Adobe Reader, which is available as a free download from the Adobe website <www.adobe.com>.

Contacting Technical Support

Family Tree Maker includes an Online Help Center that is a resource for answers to technical problems or customer service questions. You'll find easy-to-understand articles, tips, step-by-step instructions, and tools for using Family Tree Maker. To access the Help Center, select **Online Help Center** from the **Help** menu or go to <www.familytreemaker.com/support>.

If you are still having difficulties with the software, you can call 1-800-262-3787 to talk to our experienced support staff—available Monday through Friday from 10 am to 6 pm (EST). You can also e-mail your questions to support@ancestry.com.

Chapter Two
Family Tree Maker Basics

Family Tree Maker makes it easy—and enjoyable—for almost anyone to discover their family history and gather it into one convenient location. And whether you're interested in printing family charts to share at a reunion, looking for a centralized location for storing your family photos and records, or setting out to collect every fact and story about your ancestors, Family Tree Maker is the program to help you do it all.

This chapter will give you the basic skills and knowledge you need to launch the application and navigate around the software. Let's get started.

Opening and Closing Family Tree Maker

To open the program double-click the **Family Tree Maker 2011** icon on your computer desktop or click **Start>All Programs>Family Tree Maker 2011>Family Tree Maker 2011**.

When you are finished working in your tree, you can close the program. Remember, there's no need to save your tree—Family Tree Maker automatically saves changes as you make them. To close the program click **File>Exit** or click the **Close** button (**X**) in the upper-right corner of the window.

The Family Tree Maker Interface

To use any computer program effectively, the first step is to understand its unique interface and tools. You will immediately recognize many common features available in Family Tree Maker. However, there are some unique toolbars, menus, and windows you'll want to learn how to use and navigate. Once you understand the software's basic structure, you can confidently begin building your tree.

Toolbars

The main toolbar in Family Tree Maker (fig. 2-1), located at the very top of the window, is designed to provide quick navigation to various workspaces—groupings of the most important features in the software. To access a workspace, click its corresponding button on the main toolbar. For example, click the Media button to go to the Media workspace.

Figure 2-1

The main toolbar and menu bar.

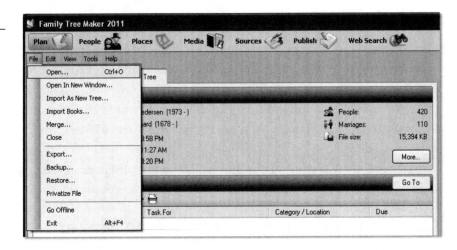

Menus and Keyboard Shortcuts

Family Tree Maker menus work like any other computer program. Simply click a menu name to display its options; then, click the option you want to use. Some menu options have keyboard shortcuts that allow you to access features and menu options without using the mouse; they are displayed next to a menu option's name (fig. 2-1).

Workspaces Overview

Family Tree Maker is organized so that you can quickly locate and use all its important features, which are grouped together in workspaces. Each workspace has a slightly different appearance and purpose, but generally, they all contain the same features, such as toolbars and tabs.

The Plan Workspace

The Plan workspace is the "control center" where you manage all of your family trees. Every time you open Family Tree Maker, this workspace will open. On the New Tree tab (fig. 2-2) you can start and import new trees; on the Current Tree tab you can view statistics about the tree you're currently working on and view your Research To-Do list.

The Plan workspace also contains the Web Dashboard, which gives you access to your Ancestry.com account information, news feeds, and online member trees.

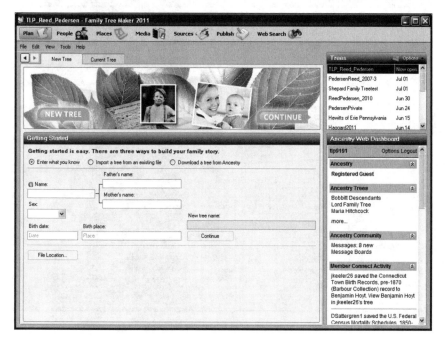

Figure 2-2

The New Tree tab on the Plan workspace.

The People Workspace

The People workspace is where you enter information about individuals and families in your tree—and where you will spend most of your time in Family Tree Maker.

The Family tab (fig. 2-3) provides a comprehensive view of your tree. You can see several generations of your family at once and easily navigate to each member of your family. Because you will use this tab often, its various sections will be explained in detail.

Figure 2-3

The Family tab on the People workspace.

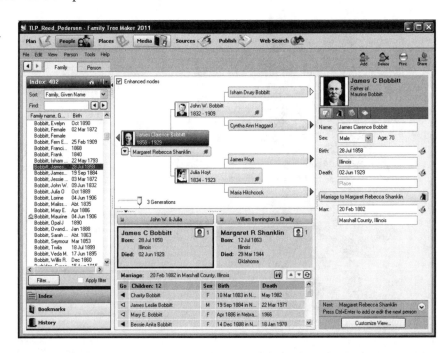

The Pedigree View

The pedigree view (fig. 2-4) helps you navigate through your family tree as well as enter new individuals. The highlighted person on the left side of the tree is the current "root" individual. "Root" simply means that this person's information and family is being displayed. To the right of the root individual you can see his or her ancestors branching out. You can click the "Enhanced nodes" checkbox to display portraits and life spans for each individual.

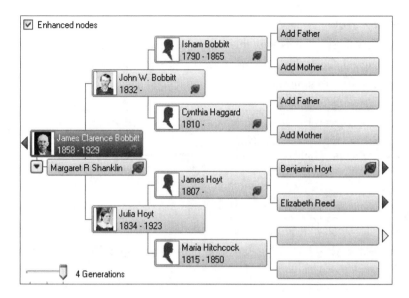

Figure 2-4

The pedigree view on the People workspace.

These buttons will help you navigate in the pedigree view:

Solid right arrow. This arrow indicates that the individual has parents (ancestors) who are not being displayed. Click this arrow to view additional generations.

White arrow. This arrow indicates that no parents (ancestors) have been entered for the individual.

Solid left arrow. This arrow appears to the left of the current root individual and indicates that he or she has children (descendants).

Left arrow. When you move your mouse over an individual's name, Family Tree Maker displays this arrow and the person's birth and death information. Click this arrow to move the individual to the root position of the pedigree view.

Down arrow. This arrow indicates that an individual has children (descendants). Click this arrow to see his or her children.

Note: If the individual has more than one spouse, the drop-down list displays only children from the individual's preferred marriage.

The Family Group View

The family group view (fig. 2-5) lets you enter a spouse and children for the current (root) individual. Click the "parent" button above an individual to display his or her parents and siblings.

Figure 2-5

The family group view on the People workspace.

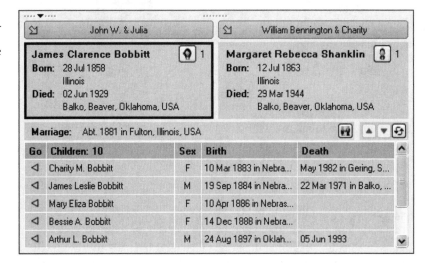

The Index Panel

The Index panel (fig. 2-6) lists all the individuals in your tree. It's one of the easiest ways to access the individual you want to focus on. To access the information for a specific individual, click on his or her name in the Index. If you

Figure 2-6

The Index panel showing the tree's home person.

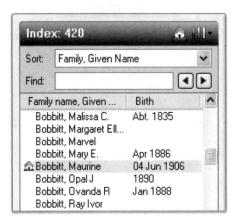

can't see the person you want, use the scroll bar to move up and down the list, or type a name in the Find field to jump to a particular person.

The house icon next to a name indicates that this individual is the home or primary person in the tree. (You'll learn more about the home person in the next chapter, "Creating a Tree.")

To make it easier to locate individuals, you can change how the Index sorts names using the **Sort** drop-down list. You can add birth, marriage, or death dates by clicking the **Show additional data** button.

You can also limit the Index so it displays only certain individuals. Simply click the **Filter** button and choose a specific family line, an individual's descendants, or a group of your choice. Click the **Bookmarks** button to see a list of individuals you have specifically bookmarked or click the **History** button to see the individuals you have most recently added or edited.

The Editing Panel

The editing panel (fig. 2-7) is where you enter basic information about an individual, such as birth, marriage, and death dates and places. The toolbar buttons let you display media items, notes, and tasks associated with the individual.

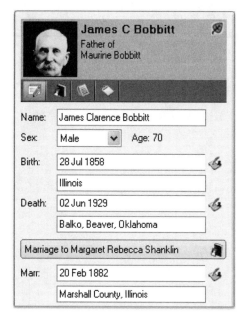

Figure 2-7

The editing panel on the People workspace.

The Person Tab

The Person tab on the People workspace (fig. 2-8) lets you add facts, media items, and notes for an individual. You can also view a timeline for an individual and their relationships to other family members.

Figure 2-8

The Person tab on the People workspace.

The Places Workspace

The Places workspace (fig. 2-9) helps you view the locations you've entered for events and individuals—and gives you the opportunity to view online maps of them, too. The Places panel on the left side shows every location you've entered in your tree. When you click on a place, it will be displayed in the map at the center of the workspace. The details panel on the right side shows the individuals who have life events associated with the location. You can also view locations as a migration path.

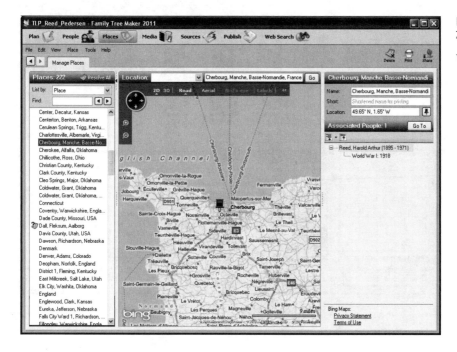

Figure 2-9

The Places workspace.

The Media Workspace

The Media workspace acts as a storage space where you keep your photos, audio recordings, movies, family documents, records, and more. On the Media Collection tab (fig. 2-10) you can view thumbnails of your media items and enter information about them. On the Media Detail tab you can add notes for an item and link them to individuals and sources.

Figure 2-10

The Collection tab on the Media workspace.

The Sources Workspace

The Sources workspace (fig. 2-11) organizes all your sources and source citations. The Source Groups panel lets you sort your sources by people, titles, and repositories, and the sources display area shows which citations have been entered for a specific source. At the bottom of the window you'll see various tabs that show the individuals linked to a source citation and let you store related notes and media items. In the Source Citation Information panel, you can enter or update specific source citations.

Figure 2-11

The Sources workspace.

The Publish Workspace

The Publish workspace offers a variety of charts and reports that you can view, print, and share. You also have the option to create family history books. The Publish Collection tab (fig. 2-12) shows the types of charts and reports that are available and an explanation of each.

Figure 2-12

The Collection tab on the Publish workspace.

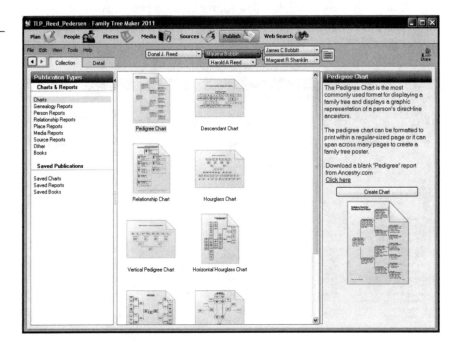

The Publish Detail tab has a display area, where you can preview a chart and any changes you've made to it. The editing panel lets you customize the chart by determining its content and format.

The Web Search Workspace

The Web Search workspace (fig. 2-13) lets you search the millions of records at Ancestry.com to find more information about your ancestors—all without leaving Family Tree Maker. You can also search other websites and easily download your discoveries into your tree.

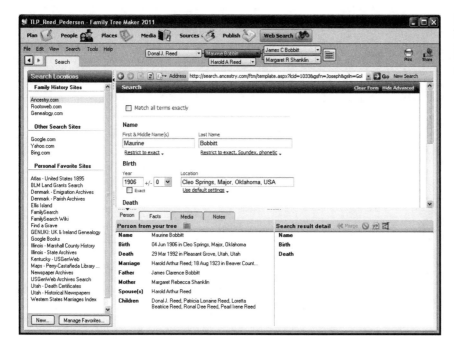

Figure 2-13

The Web Search work-space.

Chapter Three
Creating a Tree

Before You Begin

This chapter assumes that you have installed Family Tree Maker on your computer and have read chapters 1 and 2. Once you've learned a few of the basic Family Tree Maker features, you're ready to create your first tree. Make sure you have some family information to enter or have a file, such as a GEDCOM or Ancestry.com tree, ready to use.

Creating a Tree

A "tree" in Family Tree Maker is the file where you gather and enter all your family data and information. Whether you're a first-time user or you have family trees you've worked on for years, Family Tree Maker makes it easy to get started. If you have received a family history file from another family member or researcher, you can import the file, creating a new tree. You can then begin adding your own information. You can also create a tree by entering a few quick facts about an individual or by downloading a tree you've created on Ancestry.com.

Entering Your Information from Scratch

If this is your first time working on a family tree, you'll want to use this option. Enter a few brief facts about yourself and your parents, and you're on your way.

1. Click the **Plan** button on the main toolbar to open the Plan workspace.

2. On the New Tree tab, click **Enter what you know**.

3. Type your name in the **Name** field and choose your gender from the drop-down list. You can also enter your birth date and place and your parents' names.

4. Enter a name for the tree in the **New tree name** field.

5. By default, your tree will be saved to a Family Tree Maker folder located in your documents folder. If you want to save the file to another location, click **File Location** and choose a new location for your tree.

   Note: You cannot save the tree to a floppy disk or CD—your tree must be on your hard drive while you're working on it. But, you can keep a backup of your tree on a removable drive or CD.

6. Click **Continue**. The tree opens to the People workspace, where you can start entering your family information.

Importing a Tree

If you already have a file you've created or received from another family member, you can import it. You can import files from previous versions of Family Tree Maker, GEDCOM (GEnealogical Data COMmunications format) files, FamilySearch™ Personal Ancestral Files (PAFs), *Legacy Family Tree* files, and *The Master Genealogist* files.

1. If you haven't already, copy the tree you want to import to your computer's hard drive.

2. Click the **Plan** button on the main toolbar to open the Plan workspace.

3. On the New Tree tab, click **Import a tree from an existing file**.

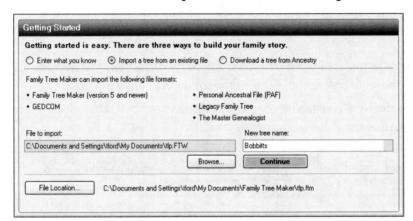

4. Click **Browse** to locate the file you want to import.

5. By default, your tree will be saved to a Family Tree Maker folder located in your documents folder. If you want to save the file to another location, click **File Location** and choose a new location for your tree.

6. If necessary, change the file's name in the **New tree name** field.

7. Click **Continue**. When the import is complete, you'll see the Import Complete window, which shows statistics for the new tree, including the number of individuals, families, and sources that were imported.

8. Click **Close**. The tree opens to the People workspace. You can start entering your family information and facts.

Downloading an Ancestry.com Family Tree

If you have a tree you've created on Ancestry.com, you can download the file and either create a new tree or merge the information with another tree. The tree will include all the facts, sources, and images you have manually attached to individuals. If you have linked Ancestry.com records to your tree, the downloaded tree will include only the information and sources associated with the records, not the actual record images.

Note: In order to download an Ancestry tree, you must be the tree's owner; even if you have been invited to view or share a tree, you will not be able to download it. If you do find a tree you want to download but don't have rights to it, consider using the Ancestry Connection Service to politely request that the owner download a GEDCOM for you.

1. Make sure you are logged in to your Ancestry.com account (if necessary click the login link in the Web Dashboard on the Plan workspace).

2. Go to the **New Tree** tab on the Plan workspace and click **Download a tree from Ancestry**. A list of your trees appears.

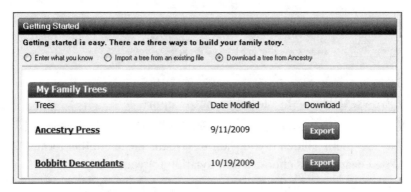

3. Click the **Export** button next to the tree you want to download.

   Note: The first time you download an Ancestry tree, you'll be prompted to identify the type of Internet connection you are using. This lets Family Tree Maker optimize the speed at which your computer transmits data.

4. Click **Download to Family Tree Maker**. A message asks you whether you want to merge the Ancestry tree with an existing tree or create a new one.

5. Click **Import** to save the file as a new tree; click **Merge** to merge the file with an existing tree.

   If you import the tree, you will be prompted to enter a name for the tree and save it; if you merge the file with an existing tree, the Merge Wizard will open and guide you through merging the trees. A message tells you when the process is complete.

How Many Trees Should You Create?

When most beginners create a family tree, their first question is, "Should I create one large, all-inclusive tree or several small trees, one for each family?" The truth is, there is no right answer. Here are some things to consider as you decide how you want to organize your trees.

The advantages to having one large tree are pretty simple. One computer file is easier to keep track of than many files—one file to enter your information in, one file to back up, one file to share. You also won't have to duplicate your efforts by entering some data, sources, and media items in multiple files.

Multiple trees can be useful too. The more trees you have, the smaller the files will typically be. If you have concerns about your computer's performance or have storage issues, smaller files might work best for you. Smaller files also make it easier to collaborate with other family members; you can send them only the family lines they're interested in.

Regardless of which way you choose to organize your trees initially, don't feel like you're stuck with a permanent decision. The flexible nature of Family Tree Maker lets you merge multiple files at any time; you can even export parts of your tree to create a brand new file.

Choosing a Primary or "Home" Person

Each tree you create will have a primary person or "home" person. By default, the home person is the first person you entered in your tree. If you're creating a tree based on your family, the home person will most likely be you. However, the home person can be anyone in your tree. Having a home person makes it easy to navigate within your tree. Get lost in a maze of ancestors? Simply click the "Go to Home Person" button on the Index panel, and you'll know right where you are again.

Occasionally, you may want to switch the home person of your tree. For example, if you're working on a specific family line, you may want to make someone in that ancestral line the home person.

There are several ways to assign a new home person. Here are the two techniques you'll most likely use.

Changing the Home Person on the Plan Workspace

1. Click the **Plan** button on the main toolbar and then click the **Current Tree** tab. At the top of the window, you'll see the name of the home person.

2. Move the mouse over "Home Person" and click the button that appears.

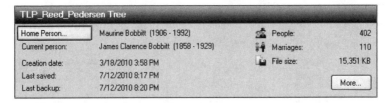

3. In the Index of Individuals window , click the name of the individual you want to be the home person and click **OK**. This individual becomes the new home person and remains the home person until you manually select a new one.

Changing the Home Person on the People Workspace

1. Click the **People** button on the main toolbar; then click the **Family** tab.

2. Find the appropriate person in the pedigree view or Index panel; then right-click the individual's name and click **Set As Home Person**.

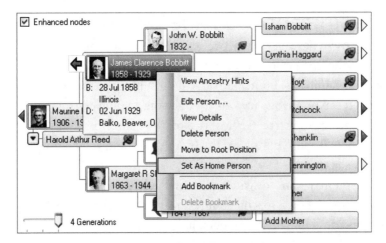

This individual becomes the new home person and remains the home person until you manually select a new one.

Part Two

Building a Tree

Chapter Four
Entering Family Information

Much of your time in Family Tree Maker will be spent entering names, dates, and events you've discovered about your family. As you begin building your tree, the best strategy is to start with what you know—basic details about yourself, your spouse, your children, and your parents. As you continue, your focus will then turn to your ancestral lines, such as your grandparents and great-grandparents.

When you've finished entering the basic birth, marriage, and death information for your family, you can expand your tree by adding details about their marriages, immigration stories, medical histories, and more.

Entering Basic Information for an Individual

On the Family tab in the People workspace, you'll begin by entering basic details about an individual in your tree, including birth and death dates.

1. Click the **People** button on the main toolbar to open the People workspace.
2. Click on an individual's name in the pedigree view. The individual's name and gender will be displayed in the editing panel. You'll enter a few basic facts here.

Entering Names

When entering names in Family Tree Maker, there are some formatting practices that will keep your names consistent and your tree organized.

Be sure to use a maiden name for a female (her last name before she was married). This practice helps you avoid confusing an individual with another person in your tree and makes it easier to trace her family.

You might encounter instances where the surname (last name) is not a single word. This is especially true with European names. You will need to identify the surname in Family Tree Maker with backslashes (\). Otherwise, Family Tree Maker will read only the last word as the surname. Here are some examples:

George \de la Vergne\   Teresa \Garcia Ramirez\

3. In the editing panel, enter a date in the **Birth Date** field.

4. Next, click the **Birth Place** field and type the name of the individual's birthplace.

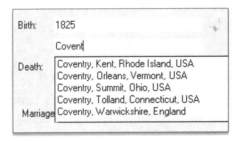

Note: As you enter a place name, you'll notice that a list of locations appears in a drop-down list. To use the suggested location, click it in the drop-down list. To ignore the suggestion, simply continue typing.

5. If you know an individual's death date and place, enter this information.

You can now continue by adding marriage facts, entering additional family members, entering facts for the individual, or even attaching photographs.

Entering Dates

Family Tree Maker automatically converts dates to the standard format used by most genealogists: day, month, year. For example, 26 Sept 1961. Usually, Family Tree Maker can figure out dates no matter how you enter them. If it cannot understand the date you enter, you will see a message that asks for clarification. Simply retype the date in the standard format.

If you don't know the date for an event, you can leave the Date field blank or type "Unknown". If you have an approximate date, you can indicate this by typing "About 1920" or "Abt. 1920".

Adding a Spouse

1. Click **Add Spouse** in the pedigree tree or the family group view. In the field that appears, enter the spouse's name (first name, middle name, and last name) and click **OK**. Don't forget to use maiden names for the females in your family.

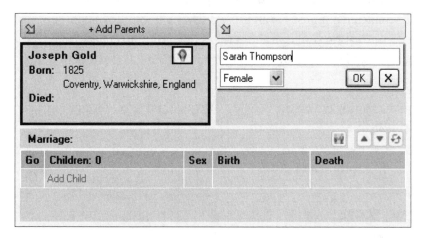

2. Choose a gender from the drop-down list and click **OK**. The spouse is now the focus of the pedigree view and editing panel.
3. Enter any basic facts (such as birth and death) you have for the individual.

Entering Locations

Recording locations consistently and completely is an important part of organizing your family history. Generally, when entering a place, you will record the location from the smallest to largest division. For example, in the United States, you would enter city or town, county, state, country (Haddam, Washington, Kansas, United States). For foreign locations, you would enter city or town, parish or district, province, country (Birmingham, West Midlands, England). You may choose to not enter a country for a location if it is the country in which you live and where most of your ancestors lived. If you do leave off country information, include this fact somewhere in your tree.

You can abbreviate place names if you want. However, make sure you use the standard abbreviations that will be recognized by others who might want to look at your research. Also, be consistent; don't spell out some place names and abbreviate others.

Entering Details About a Relationship

After you've entered a spouse for an individual, you'll want to include any additional information you have about the couple. You can enter shared facts (such as marriage or divorce), notes, and media items (such as wedding photos).

1. Go to the **Family** tab on the People workspace and select the appropriate individual.

2. If you want to enter a marriage date and place, simply enter the information in the appropriate fields.

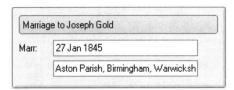

3. If you want to enter additional information for the couple, click the **Marriage to** button. The relationship window opens.

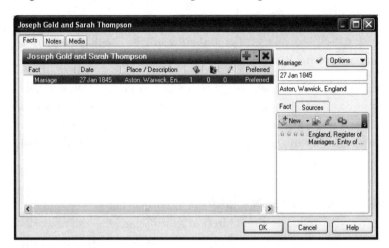

4. Click the **Facts** tab to enter facts; click the **Notes** tab to enter notes; click the **Media** tab to add photos, documents, or stories.

Adding a Child to a Family

1. In the family group view, click **Add Child**. In the field that appears, enter the child's name (first name, middle name, and last name) and click **OK**.

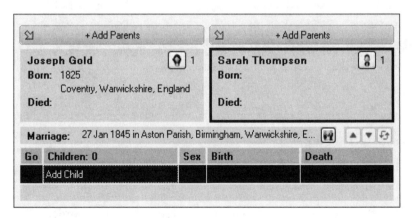

Note: Family Tree Maker assumes that the child has the same surname as the father and automatically fills in the surname for you. You can ignore the suggested name by typing over it.

2. In the editing panel, choose a gender and enter any birth and death information you have for the individual.

If you enter more children than will fit in the family group view, a scroll bar will appear and you can navigate to children not visible on the window. You can also see the total number of children entered for a couple by looking at the number to the right of the "Children" heading in the family group view.

Changing the Display Order of Children

You can change the display order of children in a family: maybe you're working on a particular individual and you want him or her to be at the top of the list, or perhaps you always want your direct ancestor to be displayed at the top of the list regardless of his or her birth order.

1. Go to the **Family** tab on the People workspace and select the appropriate family.

2. Click the child's name in the family group view.

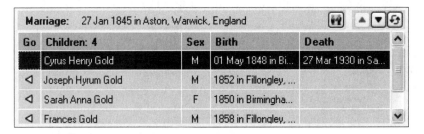

3. Do one of these options:

   • Click the **Move up** and **Move down** buttons to move a child to a specific place in the order.

   • Click the **Sort** button to display the children in their birth order.

Adding Parents

In addition to entering information about your immediate family, you can add multiple generations of a family—grandparents, great-grandparents, aunts and uncles, and so on.

1. Go to the **Family** tab on the People workspace. In the Index panel or pedigree view, click the name of the individual you want to add a father or mother to.

2. Click **Add Father** or **Add Mother** in the pedigree view.

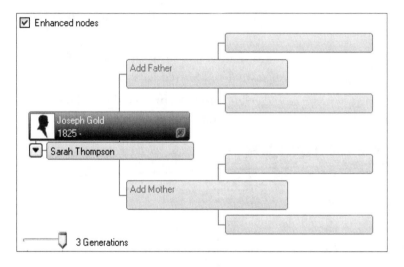

3. Enter the parent's name (first name, middle name, and last name). Don't forget to use maiden names for the females in your family.

4. In the editing panel, choose a gender and enter any birth and death information you have for the individual.

Adding More Details

So far, you've only entered general family relationships in the People workspace on the Family tab. You might have noticed that the People workspace contains another tab, the Person tab. You can use this tab to enter, edit, and delete additional facts about an individual.

Adding a Fact

In addition to events such as birth and death, you can add many facts you've learned about an individual. Some examples include christenings, education, immigration, and occupations.

Note: For each fact you'll want to record the "source" of the information. A source is any material where you find information related to the fact or event, such as a book, database, or person. For more information see chapter 5, "Documenting Your Research."

1. Go to the **Person** tab on the People workspace and select the appropriate individual.

2. Click the **Facts** button. The information you've already entered for the individual appears in the Individual and Shared Facts section.

3. Right-click the workspace and select **Add Fact**, or click the **Add fact** (+) button in the toolbar. The Add Fact window opens.

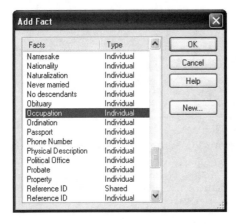

4. Choose a fact from the list and click **OK**.

Note: If the fact you want to use is not in the list (for example, college graduation), you can add it by clicking the **New** button in the Add Fact window. Family Tree Maker adds the new fact to the list for future use.

Notice that the editing panel on the right-hand side of the window displays the appropriate fields for the fact.

5. Complete the **Date**, **Place**, and **Description** fields as necessary.

Note: Don't forget to add a source for the fact. For instructions on adding a source, see "Creating Sources" on page 62.

Commonly Used Facts

In addition to birth, marriage, and death facts, here are some facts you will probably encounter as you record your family history:

- **Address.** Addresses can be useful for recording contact information for living relatives or recording the area where an ancestor lived.

- **Also Known As.** If an individual was known by a nickname rather than his or her given name, you'll want to record this name in order to distinguish the individual from others in your tree.

- **Cause of Death.** Knowing your family's health history may help you prevent and treat illnesses that run in family lines. You can record an individual's cause of death or enter any details you feel are important about the individual's medical history, from long-term illness to simple things such as "suffers from allergies."

- **Christening.** Birth records are not always available for individuals in your tree; therefore, christening records become useful because they may be the earliest available information you can find for an ancestor.

- **Emigration/ Immigration.** Emigration and immigration records are the first step in finding your ancestors in their homeland. Use these facts to record dates, ports of departure and arrival, and even ship names.

- **Physical Description.** Although not necessarily beneficial to your research, a physical description can be a fascinating addition to any family history.

- **Title.** If an individual has a title, such as Captain, you'll want to record this information in order to distinguish the individual from others in your tree.

Adding Alternate Facts

You may have conflicting information about the same life event (e.g., two different birth dates). Multiple facts for the same event are referred to as "alternate facts" in Family Tree Maker. You should record facts *and* alternate facts in your tree. This is especially valuable if you are unsure which fact is correct. Creating an alternate fact is the same process as adding another fact, and both facts will appear side-by-side in the Individual and Shared Facts section. When you have two facts for an item, one fact will be "preferred," meaning it will be included in charts and reports, and one fact will not. In this example, the birth fact has one preferred fact and one alternate fact.

Choosing a Preferred Fact

If you enter multiple facts for the same event, you will have to choose a preferred fact. Typically, this is the fact that you believe to be most accurate or complete. Once you mark a fact as preferred, it will be the default fact displayed in the various views, charts, and reports.

1. Go to the **Person** tab on the People workspace and select the appropriate individual.

2. Click the **Facts** button; then click the fact that you want to make the preferred fact.

3. In the editing panel, click the **Options** button and choose **Preferred** from the drop-down list.

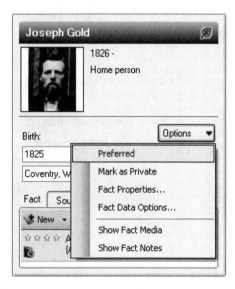

The Preferred column in the Individual and Shared Facts section now shows the fact as preferred.

TIP

You can also set a preferred fact by right-clicking the fact and choosing **Set As Preferred** from the drop-down list.

Making a Fact Private

You may enter facts about an individual that you do not want to share with other family members or researchers. If you make a fact "private," you can choose whether or not to include the information in reports or when you export a tree.

1. Go to the **Person** tab on the People workspace and select the appropriate individual.

2. Click the **Facts** button; then click the fact that you want to make private.

3. In the editing panel, click the **Options** button and choose **Mark as Private** from the drop-down list.

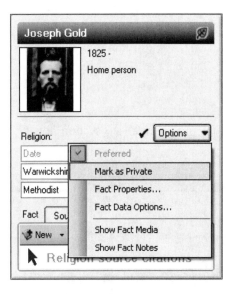

A lock icon appears next to the fact in the Facts section.

A lock icon indicates that this fact has been marked as private.

Individual Facts		
Address	1851	Little Ann, Birmingham, England
Baptism	12 Sep 1825	Coventry, Warwickshire, England
Birth	Abt. 1826	Coventry, Warwick, England
Religion	1865	Warwickshire, England; Methodist
Residence	1845	Fillongley, Warwick, England

Adding a Note for an Individual

You may have family stories, legends, or research resources that you want to refer to occasionally. Family Tree Maker lets you enter this detailed information in "notes"—up to 1MB of space, or about 200 printed pages, per note.

> **TIP**
>
> If you are entering notes from another document on your computer, you can usually "copy and paste" so you don't have to retype existing text. For instance, you could copy text from a Word document and then paste it into the Notes tab.

Entering a Personal Note

Personal notes might be as simple as a physical description of an individual or as lengthy as a transcript of an interview with your grandmother.

Note: You should *not* record source information on the Notes tab; if you do, the information won't be included in source reports.

1. Go to the **Person** tab on the People workspace and select the appropriate individual.

2. Click the **Notes** tab at the bottom of the Person tab. Then click the **Person note** button in the Notes toolbar.

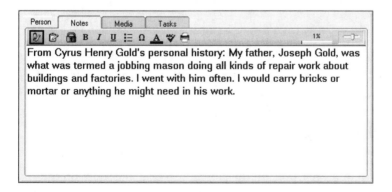

3. Place your cursor in the notes area and enter the text you want to include for the individual. If a word doesn't fit at the end of a line, Family Tree Maker automatically moves it to the beginning of the next line. You should press **Enter** only when you reach the end of a paragraph.

Note: You'll notice that there's no Save button on the Notes tab; Family Tree Maker automatically saves notes as you enter them.

Entering a Research Note

Many times when you find a record or learn a new fact about someone in your tree, you will discover clues that can help you learn more about your family. You can create research notes to remind you of the next steps you want to take.

1. Go to the **Person** tab on the People workspace and select the appropriate individual.

2. Click the **Notes** tab at the bottom of the Person tab. Then click the **Research note** button in the Notes toolbar.

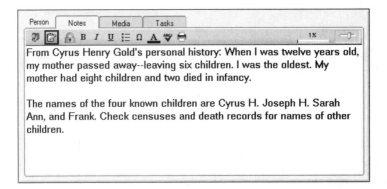

3. Place your cursor in the notes area and enter the text you want to include for the individual.

Changing a Note's Display Size

You can resize your notes to make the text larger and easier to read or make the text smaller to fit more words on the tab. Simply drag the slider on the right side of the notes toolbar to make the text larger or smaller. When you resize a note, it changes the display only; it does not affect permanent settings or the print size of a note.

Making a Note Private

You may have information about an individual that you do not want to share with other family members or researchers. If you make a note "private," you can choose whether or not you want to include it in reports or when you export your tree.

After entering a note, click the **Toggle private** button. You can tell the note has been marked as private because the lock icon has a yellow box around it.

Printing a Note

To print an individual note, click the printer icon on the Notes toolbar. Select your printing options and click **OK**. You can also create a report of all research notes you've entered and print it. (Go to the Publish workspace and choose **Person Reports**. Then double-click **Research Note Report**.)

Creating Smart Stories™

Smart Stories is a narrative tool that can help you record family stories quickly by selecting facts, sources, and notes you've already entered in your tree; then you can drag and drop them into a special text item called a Smart Story. And best of all, Smart Story text is linked to your tree. So if you find out that Grandpa's birth date is different than you thought, you can change it in your tree and the text will be updated automatically. You can create two types of Smart Stories:

- **Media items.** A media Smart Story is a text file that exist outside your tree and is linked to a specific individual. You can share it with others or export it with your tree, and if you upload your tree to Ancestry.com it will be included.

- **Publications.** A publication Smart Story is a document that exists only inside your tree and is not linked to a specific individual. If you upload your tree to Ancestry.com, this type of Smart Story won't be included.

Note: You can edit Smart Stories. Simply double-click the text or right-click and choose "Change to free form text." However, text will no longer be linked to your tree and will not be updated if you make changes.

Starting a Smart Story

You can start a Smart Story in two ways:

- If you want to create a Smart Story as a media item, go to an individual's Person tab. Then click the **Media** tab at the bottom of the window. Click **New** and choose **Create New Smart Story** from the drop-down list.

  You have the option of starting with a blank page or letting Family Tree Maker create a story for you using an individual's preferred facts and portrait.

- If you want to create a Smart Story as a publication, go to the **Collection** tab on the Publish workspace. In **Publication Types**, click **Other**. Double-click the **Smart Story** icon, or select its icon and then click the **Detail** tab.

  Note: To access a Smart Story you've saved, go to the Publish workspace. In Saved Publications, click **Saved Reports**.

Inserting a Short Biography

1. Place your cursor on the page where you want to add a biography. Then choose "Personal Biography" from the drop-down list in the Smart Stories toolbar.

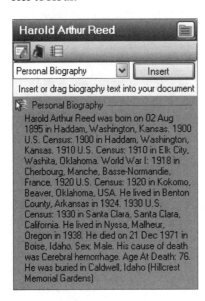

2. Drag the text to your document or click **Insert**.

    You can tell which text is linked to your tree. Move the cursor over the text; Smart Stories text will be highlighted.

    Harold Arthur Reed was born 02 Aug 1895 in Haddam, Washington, Kansas. 1900 U.S. Census: 1900 in Haddam, Washington, Kansas. 1910 U.S. Census: 1910 in Elk City, Washita, Oklahoma. World War I: 1918 in Cherbourg, Manche, Basse-Normandie, France. 1920 U.S. Census: 1920 in Kokomo, Beaver, Oklahoma, USA. He lived in Benton County, Arkansas in 1924. 1930 U.S. Census: 1930 in Santa Clara, Santa Clara, California. He lived in Nyssa, Malheur, Oregon in 1938. He died on 21 Dec 1971 in Boise, Idaho. Sex Male. His cause of death was Cerebral hemorrhage. Age At Death: 76. He was buried in Caldwell, Idaho (Hillcrest Memorial Gardens) He lived in Benton County, Arkansas in 1924

Inserting Facts

1. Place your cursor on the page where you want to add a fact. Then choose "Facts" from the drop-down list in the Smart Stories toolbar.

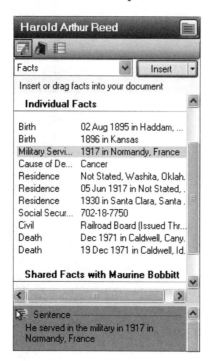

2. Click the fact you want to add to your story. Below the fact, you'll see options of how the fact will be entered. You can choose to create a sentence or add specific details.

3. Drag the text to your document or click **Insert**.

Inserting Sources

1. Place your cursor on the page where you want to add a source. Then choose "Fact Sources" from the drop-down list in the Smart Stories toolbar.

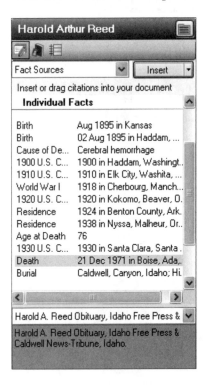

2. Click the fact that has the source you want to add to your story. Below you'll see any associated source citations. If more than one source citation exists for a fact, you can choose it from a drop-down list.

3. Drag the text to your document or click **Insert**.

Inserting Notes

1. Place your cursor on the page where you want to add person notes you've entered for an individual. Then choose "Notes" from the options drop-down list.

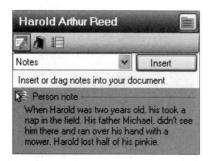

2. Drag the text to your document or click **Insert**.

Adding Media Items to Smart Stories

1. Place your cursor on the page where you want to add the media item. Then click the **Media** button on the Smart Stories toolbar.

2. Click the media item you want.

3. Drag the image to your document or click **Insert**.

Creating Smart Stories Timelines

You can use facts in a person's life and historical events to create a timeline.

1. Place your cursor on the page where you want to create the timeline. Then click the **Timeline** button on the Smart Stories toolbar.

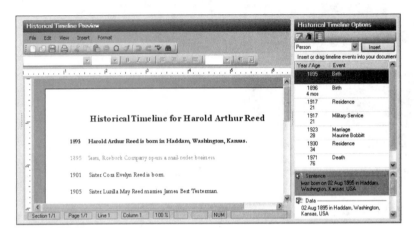

2. Click the event you want to add to your story. Below the event, you'll see options of how the event will be entered. You can create a sentence or add specific details.

3. Drag the text to your document or click **Insert**.

Working with Relationships

As you dig deeper into your family history you will discover mothers who die in childbirth, fathers who remarry, adoptions, and other unique situations. Family Tree Maker can handle all different types of relationships.

Viewing an Individual's Family Relationships

You can see all the members of an individual's family at a glance—spouses, children, parents, and siblings.

1. Go to the **Person** tab on the People workspace and select the appropriate individual.

2. Click the **Relationships** button. You can now see parents, siblings, spouses, and children entered for the individual.

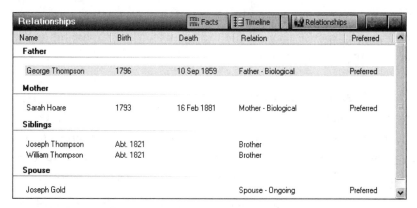

Adding Additional Spouses

If an individual in your family has been married more than once, you can enter the additional spouse and marriage information.

1. Go to the **Person** tab on the People workspace and select the appropriate individual.

2. In the family group view, click the **Spouse** icon next to the individual. From the drop-down list, you have the choice of accessing the information for an existing spouse or creating information for a new spouse.

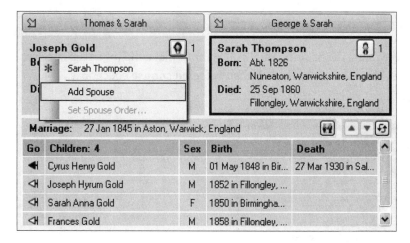

3. Choose **Add Spouse** from the drop-down list.

4. Enter the name of the new spouse and click **OK**. Family Tree Maker displays a new family group view—this time with the new spouse.

5. To view the first spouse again, click the **Spouse** icon and choose his or her name from the drop-down list.

Choosing a "Preferred" Spouse

If you enter more than one spouse for an individual, you need to indicate who is the preferred spouse. (Usually this is the spouse whose children are in your direct family line.) The preferred spouse will become the default spouse displayed in the family group view, pedigree view, and charts and reports.

1. Go to the **Family** tab on the People workspace and select the appropriate individual.

2. Click the **Person** tab and then click the **Relationships** button. You should see two names listed under the Spouses heading.

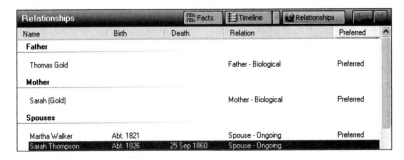

3. Click the name of the individual you want to make the preferred spouse. Then, in the editing panel, click the **Preferred spouse** checkbox.

Switching Between Multiple Spouses

You can view the information and children of only one spouse at a time, so you may need to switch between multiple spouses when you want to work with a specific family. You will also need to change spouses if you want to add information about that particular marriage.

1. Go to the **Family** tab on the People workspace and select the appropriate individual.

2. In the family group view, click the **Spouse** button next to the individual. From the drop-down list, choose the other spouse.

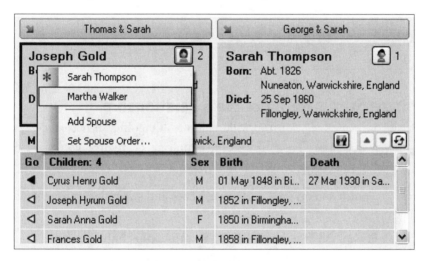

The family group view now displays the individual and the alternate spouse you have selected. After making any necessary edits to this alternate spouse, click the **Spouse** button again to select the alternate spouse.

Choosing a Type of Relationship for a Couple

You can choose what type of relationship a couple has with each other (e.g., partner, friend, spouse).

1. Go to the **Family** tab on the People workspace and select the appropriate individual.

2. Click the **Person** tab and then click the **Relationships** button.

3. Click the spouse's name. Then, in the editing panel, choose a relationship type from the **Relationship** drop-down list.

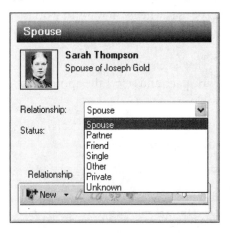

Choosing a Status for a Couple's Relationship

The status of a couple's relationship will default to "Ongoing." If necessary, you can change this status. For example, if a couple gets a divorce, you can indicate this with their relationship status.

1. Go to the **Family** tab on the People workspace and select the appropriate individual.

2. Click the **Person** tab and then click the **Relationships** button.

3. Click the spouse's name. Then, in the editing panel, choose a status from the **Status** drop-down list.

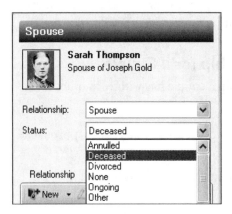

Choosing a Relationship Between Parents and a Child

You can indicate a child's relationship to each of his or her parents (e.g., natural, adopted, foster).

1. Go to the **Family** tab on the People workspace and select the appropriate individual.

2. Click the **Person** tab and then click the **Relationships** button.

3. Click the father or mother's name. Then, in the editing panel, choose a relationship from the **Relationship** drop-down list.

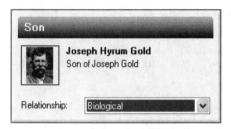

Adding an Unrelated Individual

During your family research, you might discover a person that you think is related to your family, but you have no proof. You will still want to add this person to your tree so you can keep track of his or her information. Family Tree Maker lets you add individuals without having to link them to other family members in your tree. And if you find out that they are part of your family, you can easily link them in.

1. Click the **People** button on the main toolbar.

2. Click **Person>Add Person>Add Unrelated Person**.

3. Enter the person's name (first, middle, and last). Then choose a gender from the drop-down list and click **OK**.

Viewing Timelines

Timelines can be a great tool to put the life of your ancestor in context—historical and otherwise. Family Tree Maker lets you view three timeline variations: events in an individual's life; events in an individual's life and important events in his or her immediate family (such as birth, marriage, and death); events in an individual's life and historical events.

Viewing an Individual's Timeline

You can view a timeline of all the events you've entered for an individual. Each life event is represented by a horizontal bar showing its date and location and the person's age at the time.

1. Go to the **Person** tab on the People workspace and select the appropriate person.

2. Click the **Timeline** button.

Including Family Events in a Timeline

You can view an individual's life events shown side-by-side in a timeline with the births, marriages, and deaths of immediate family members—spouses, children, and parents.

1. To display the individual's life along with family events, click the down arrow next to the **Timeline** button and select **Show Family Events**.

Events in an individual's life are indicated by green markers, and events in his or her family's life are indicated by pink markers.

2. To return to a timeline of just the individual's life, click the same arrow and deselect **Show Family Events**.

Including Historical Events in a Timeline

You can view an individual's life in the context of significant historical events.

Note: Family Tree Maker comes with a set of default historical events that you can edit, delete, and add to. To learn more, see "Managing Historical Events" on page 250.

1. To display the individual's life along with historical events, click the down arrow next to the **Timeline** button and select **Show Historical Events**.

Events in an individual's life are indicated by green markers, and historical events are indicated by yellow markers.

2. If you want to learn more about a historical event, click the event. A description appears on the right side of the window.

3. To return to a timeline of just the individual's life, click the same arrow and deselect **Show Historical Events**.

Chapter Five
Documenting Your Research

Documenting sources—recording where you discovered a fact about your family—is one of the most important aspects of your research. Sources are valuable for many reasons. When you cite a source, you are proving to others which records you based your facts on; if you eventually share your research with your family or other researchers, your family history will be judged for accuracy based on your sources. And if your sources are detailed and correct, others will be able to follow your research footsteps.

Each time you add information to your tree, you'll want to create a source and source citation that describe where you found the information. For example, if you find your father's birthplace on his World War I draft card, you'll want to include this information in your tree when you record his birth date and birthplace. If you discover your great-grandfather's will that lists the names of all his children, you'll want to create a source for this document.

Understanding Sources and Source Citations

If you're new to family history, you may not be familiar with sources and source citations. This section gives an explanation of each and also shows you some examples.

- A source contains unchanging facts about an item; for example, the author, title, and publication information for a book.

- Source citations are individual details that explain where you found a fact, such as the page number in a book.

To help you understand how sources and source citations work together, let's look at an example from the 1930 United States Federal Census. First, you would create a source for the census that would include information like this:

- A title—1930 United States Federal Census

- Where you located the source—www.ancestry.com

- Publishing details—Original data: United States of America, Bureau of the Census. Washington, D.C.: National Archives and Records Administration, 1930.

As you can see, this basic information about the 1930 census won't change regardless of who you find in the records. However, because you'll find different families and individuals in different locations throughout the census, the census fact for each person will need its own source citation. A source citation for an individual you found in the 1930 census might include this information:

- Source—1930 United States Federal Census

- Citation text—Harold Reed household, Santa Clara Township, Santa Clara County, California. Roll: 219; Page: 14A; Enumeration district: 110.

A source citation for a different individual might look like this. (Notice the source is the same as the previous example.)

- Source—1930 United States Federal Census

- Citation text—Michael Reed household, Kokomo Township, Beaver County, Oklahoma. Roll: 1892; Page: 5B; Enumeration district: 26.

Both individuals can be found in the 1930 census (the source), but the source citation for each individual has changed because the individuals were located in different places in the source.

Creating Sources

If you find your grandparents' marriage date in the family Bible, you should create a source for that Bible. If you find the image of a death record for your great-aunt in an online database, you should create a source for that database.

Family Tree Maker lets you create sources in two ways: using templates or a basic format. Source templates are useful because you don't have to guess which details need to be entered. Choose the type of source you're creating (for example, for an obituary), and Family Tree Maker displays the relevant fields. If you don't want to use a template (for example, because you prefer to use your own system of citation or you can't find a template that matches the item you're sourcing), you can create a source by simply completing the standard fields (such as author, title, and publisher) in the basic source format.

Adding a Source for a Fact

You will usually add a source as you create a source citation for a fact or event you are entering in your tree. This section focuses on adding a source while entering facts on the Family tab in the People workspace.

Note: You need to create only one source for each item; you can use a source for as many source citations as necessary.

1. Go to the **Family** tab on the People workspace.
2. In the editing panel, click the **New source citation** button next to the fact you want to add a source to. Then choose **Add New Source Citation** from the drop-down list.

3. The Add Source Citation window opens. If you want to create a source using a template, continue with the next task, "Creating a Source from a Template"; if you want to create your own source, continue with "Creating a Source Using the Basic Format" on page 67.

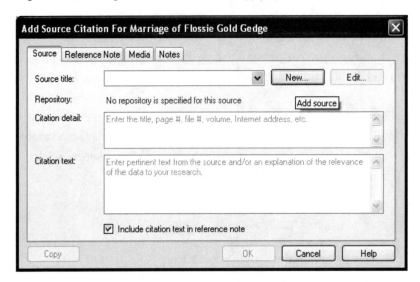

Using Source Templates

Family Tree Maker includes more than 170 source templates to help you source everything from homemade samplers and online databases to vital records. The source templates are based on the QuickCheck models used in Elizabeth Shown Mills's book *Evidence Explained*—the premier reference for citing genealogy sources.

Creating a Source from a Template

Using a source template is simple. To determine which template you should use for a specific record, you can enter keywords and choose from a list of suggestions, or you can view a list of all the available templates and choose the one that fits best.

To choose a template using keywords

1. Access the Add Source Citation window and click **New**. (If you need help, see "Adding a Source for a Fact" on page 63.) The Add Source window opens.

2. Enter a keyword in the **Source template** field and choose a template from the drop-down list. To narrow the list, enter multiple keywords. For example, "property" brings up eleven results, while "property grant" brings up one result.

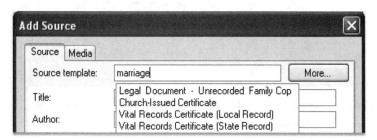

3. The fields that appear now reflect the template you've chosen. Complete these fields as necessary and click **OK**.

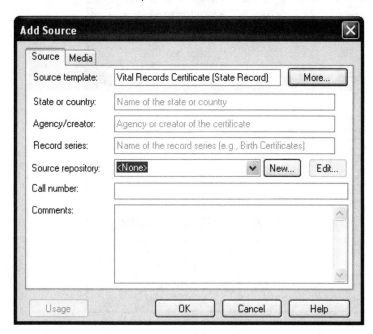

You can now add a source citation for the fact (see page 69).

To choose a template from a list

1. Access the Add Source Citation window and click **New**. (If you need help, see "Adding a Source for a Fact" on page 63.) The Add Source window opens.

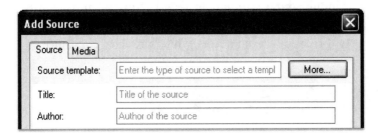

2. Click **More**.

3. In **Source group**, choose the group that most closely matches the item you're sourcing. The categories list changes to reflect the selected source group.

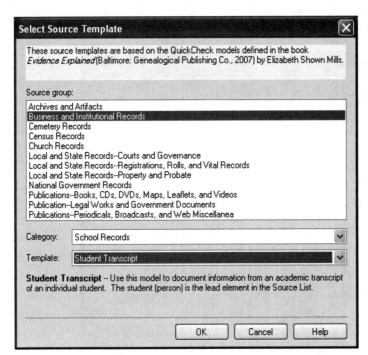

4. Choose the appropriate category from the **Category** drop-down list. The templates list changes to reflect the selected source group and category.

5. Choose a template from the **Template** drop-down list. A description of the template is displayed beneath its title.

6. Click **OK** to return to the Add Source window; the fields that appear now reflect the template you've chosen. Complete these fields as necessary and click **OK**. You can now add a source citation for the fact (see page 69).

Creating a Source Using the Basic Format

If you don't want to use source templates, you can create a source by simply completing some standard fields (such as author, title, and publisher) on the basic source format.

1. Access the Add Source Citation window and click **New**. (If you need help, see "Adding a Source for a Fact" on page 63.) The Add Source window opens.

2.   Complete the source fields as necessary:

- **Title.** Enter the title of the source exactly as it appears in the source.

- **Author.** Enter the author or originator's name.

- **Publisher name.** Enter the name of the publishing company.

- **Publisher location.** Enter the place of publication (for example, London, England).

- **Publish date.** Enter the copyright date for the source (usually only a year).

- **Source repository.** Create a new repository or choose one from the drop-down list.

   A repository is the location where an original source exists. This could be a library, archive, county courthouse, or cousin's home, for example. To create a repository, click **New**. Then enter the name, address, and phone number for the location. You can also add an e-mail address, if one exists.

- **Call number.** Enter a call number, if one exists.

   The call number is the number assigned to the source at the repository where you found the item. It could be a microfilm number, a Dewey Decimal system number, or some other numbering system unique to a particular library or archive.

- **Comments.** Enter any comments about the source and the information found in it. This information will not print on your reports; it is for your personal reference. You might include a description of the item or even information about its legibility.

3.   Click **OK.** You can now add a source citation for the fact (see page 69).

Creating Source Citations

After you have created a source you are ready to identify where in the source you found information—by creating a source citation. Family Tree Maker lets you create source citations in a variety of ways. As you cite each fact you'll need to decide which method is most effective in that situation. If you're adding a source you've never used before, you'll want to create a new source citation. If you have already created a source citation (for example, for a census record), you don't need to create another citation; simply link the fact to the citation you've already created.

> Note: You can have more than one source citation for the same fact. For example, you might find an immigration date for your great-grandmother on a naturalization record and a census record. You can add source citations for both records.

Adding a New Source Citation

Every time you add a fact to your tree, you should take a minute to document where you discovered the information, whether it's a book in a library, a record you located online, or a photograph you discovered in an old trunk. When you create a new source citation, you'll link it to the appropriate source and then add any additional identifying information such as page number, volume number, or explanatory text.

1. Access the Add Source Citation window. (If you need help, see "Adding a Source for a Fact" on page 63.)

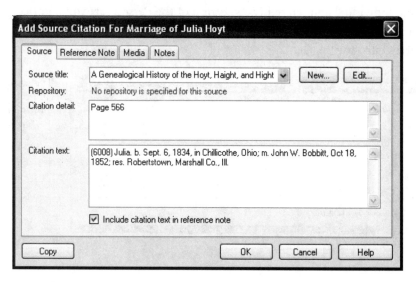

2. Change the citation as necessary:

- **Source title.** From the drop-down list, choose the source where you found the information.

- **Citation detail.** Enter specific details about where you found the information, such as the page or volume number or website address.

- **Citation text.** Enter any additional information. For example, you might enter a quote from a book or add a paraphrased summary of the source text.

- **Include citation text in reference note.** Click this checkbox to include text in the Citation text field in printed reference notes. If this text is just for your own information, make sure the checkbox is not selected. (The source title and citation detail are automatically included in printed reference notes.)

You can include a media item or note as part of a source citation. For instructions see "Attaching a Media Item to a Source Citation" on page 74, and "Adding a Note to a Source Citation" on page 75.

3. Click **OK**.

In the Individual and Shared Facts section of the Person tab, you'll notice that the sources column contains a number, indicating that you have sources cited for the fact.

The sources column is indicated by a scroll icon.

Linking a Fact to an Existing Source Citation

If you have already created a citation for a specific source, such as a death certificate, you don't have to create a new source citation for each fact or individual that is included in this source; you can use the existing citation. For example, if you find information about your grandparents in your aunt's death certificate (such as their names and birthplaces), you don't have to create a new source citation for the death certificate again; you can simply link to the citation you already created.

1. Go to the **Person** tab on the People workspace and select the appropriate individual.

2. Click the **Facts** button. Then click the fact you want to add a source citation to.

3. On the **Sources** tab, click the **New** button and choose **Use Existing Source Citation** from the drop-down list.

The Find Source Citation window opens.

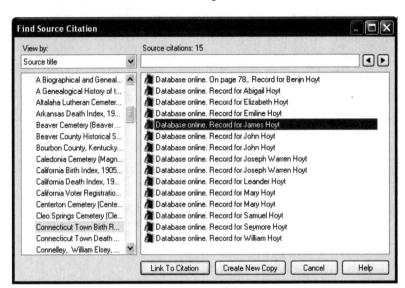

4. Click the citation you want to link to from the list.

5. Click **Link to Citation**. The citation information now appears on the Sources tab.

Copying and Updating a Source Citation

If you have a source citation that is similar to one you need, you don't have to create a brand new citation. Simply create a copy of the source citation and change the relevant details (such as the page or volume number). For example, if you find several family members in the same city directory for Cleveland, Ohio, you can create a source citation for one family and then copy and update the source citation for every family that shows up in the same directory.

1. Go to the **Person** tab on the People workspace and select the appropriate individual.

2. Click the **Facts** button. Then click the fact that you want to add a source citation to.

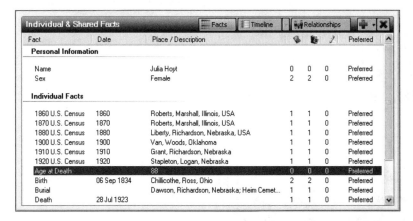

3. On the **Sources** tab, click the **New** button and choose **Use Existing Source Citation** from the drop-down list. The Find Source Citation window opens.

4. Click the citation you want to copy from the list.

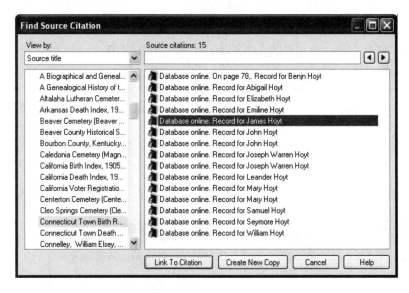

5.   Click **Create New Copy**. A citation link appears on the Sources tab on the Person page.

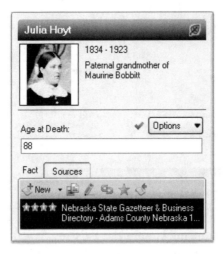

Now you can edit the citation without affecting the original.

6.   Double-click the source citation to open it in an editing window. Then make any necessary changes and click **OK**.

Attaching a Media Item to a Source Citation

If you have an image or recording of a source, you can link it to a source citation. For example, you might have a scan of a marriage certificate or census record that you want to include with the source citation.

Note: If you link the source to a media item that isn't already in your tree, the item will be added to the tree's Media workspace.

1.   Click the **Media** tab in a source citation.

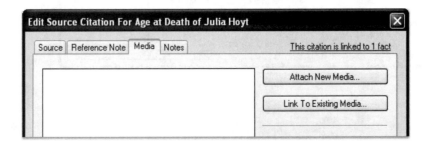

2. Do one of these options:

   - If the media item you want is already in your tree, click **Link to Existing Media**. Click the item you want; then click **OK**.

   - If you want to add a media item, click **Attach New Media**. Use the file management window to navigate to the media item you want. Then click **Open**.

3. Click **OK**.

Adding a Note to a Source Citation

You can use the Notes tab to include any additional information you have about a source that you weren't able to include elsewhere. For example, you can enter a note about how you discovered a source or where the source is located.

1. Click the **Notes** tab in a source citation.
2. Enter a note. The notes are automatically saved.

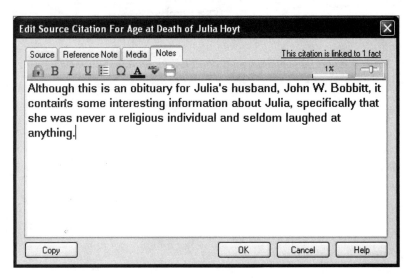

3. Click **OK**.

Chapter Six
Including Media Items

As you gather names, dates, and facts, you'll realize that these tell only part of your family's story. In order to really bring your ancestors to life, you'll want to illustrate your family history with photographs, important documents, and video and sound clips.

Family Tree Maker helps you organize your multimedia items all in one central location. You can link media items to specific individuals; record important notes and information about the items; use the images in selected trees, reports, and charts; and more.

What Media Items Can I Add to My Tree?

Photographs are usually the first thing that comes to mind when you want to illustrate your family history. But don't limit yourself; many personal objects can be scanned or photographed. Here are some ideas of items you might want to include:

- Important records, such as birth and marriage certificates, censuses, passports, diplomas, obituaries, and Bibles.
- Photographs of heirlooms or items with sentimental value, such as jewelry, medals, trophies, artwork, quilts, christening outfits, and furniture.
- Images of ancestral houses and hometowns, businesses, maps, cemeteries, and headstones.
- Family documents, such as letters, funeral books, diaries, Christmas cards, awards, and newspaper and magazine articles.
- Sound clips of favorite songs, bedtime stories, and oral histories.

Adding Media Items

You can add photos, images, sound files, videos, scanned documents, and more to an individual. For example, if you have a baby photo of your grandfather or a photo of his military uniform, you'll want to add it to his Media tab. You can add items that are already on your computer or you can scan items directly into Family Tree Maker.

Adding a Media Item for an Individual

1. Go to the **Person** tab on the People workspace and select the appropriate individual.

2. Click the **Media** tab at the bottom of the window.

3. Click the **New** button and choose **Add New Media** from the drop-down list.

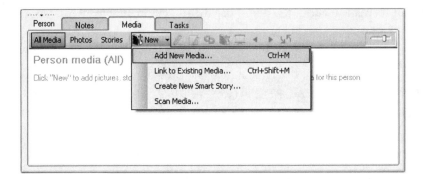

4. Use the file management window to navigate to the media item you want to add to your tree. Then click **Open**.

> **TIP**
>
> In the file management window, you can select multiple media items by clicking on each file you want while holding down the CTRL key.

A message asks whether you want to link the file(s) to your tree or create a copy of the file(s).

5. Click **Copy this file** to create an additional copy of the file in a Family Tree Maker media folder, or click **Link to this file** to leave the file where it is on your computer.

> **TIP**
>
> You might want to add copies of your media items to the Media folder so that all your heritage photos and other media items are gathered into one central location on your computer. This makes them easier to find and easier to back up as a group.

6. Click the checkbox for the category you want this item to belong to; you can select multiple categories. (For more information about categories, see "Media Categories" on page 87.)

7. Click **OK**. The item is added to the individual's Media tab.

   Note: When you add a picture or other media item to Family Tree Maker, the original file is not moved from its location on your computer.

Scanning an Image into Your Tree

If you have images you'd like to include in your tree that aren't already on your computer's hard drive, you don't have to scan the items to your computer and manually add them into your tree; you can scan them directly into your tree.

When you scan an image, you can choose the resolution in which the item will be saved. The higher the resolution, or DPI (dots per inch), the sharper your image will look—and the larger the file size that will be created. If you plan on viewing your images online or sharing them via e-mail, you'll want to scan images at a lower resolution such as 72 to 150 DPI; if you want to print images in charts and reports, you'll want to use a higher resolution such as 200 to 300 DPI.

1. Make sure your scanner is connected to your computer and turned on.

2. Go to the Media workspace and choose **Media>Scan Media**. Family Tree Maker automatically searches for connected scanners.

3. Change any scanner settings and click **Scan**. The image is added to the Media workspace.

Entering Details for a Media Item

After you add a media item, it's a good idea to enter details about it such as a caption, date, and description.

1. Go to the **Collection** tab on the Media workspace. Double-click the media item you want to add details to, or click the image and then click the **Detail** tab.

2. Change the image's details as necessary:

    •   **Caption.** Enter a brief title for the item.

    •   **Date.** Enter a date for the photo. (Normally this would be the date of origin for the item.)

    •   **Description.** Describe the media item in detail. For photos you may want to enter the names of individuals or information about the location depicted; for heirlooms you may want to explain what the item is and its significance to your family.

3. To assign the item to a category, click the **Edit** button next to the **Categories** field. Mark the checkbox for the category you want this item to belong to; you can select multiple categories. Then click **OK**.

Note: The Filename and Location field shows the file name of the media item and where it is located on your computer. You can click the location link to open the folder in which the media item resides.

Entering a Note About a Media Item

If you have additional information that won't fit in a media item's description, you can enter it in the item's notes. For example, a photo of your grandmother in her graduation robes may include notes about her college education and how you came in possession of the image.

1. Go to the **Collection** tab on the Media workspace. Double-click the media item you want to add a note to, or click the image and then click the **Detail** tab.

2. Click the **Notes** tab at the bottom of the window.

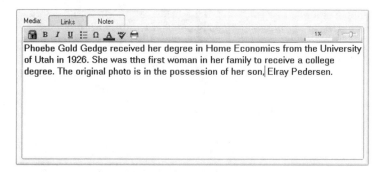

3. Place the cursor in the text area and enter the information. Notes are automatically saved as you type.

Note: For more information about using notes in Family Tree Maker, see "Adding a Note for an Individual" on page 45.

Assigning a Portrait to an Individual

You can decide which image will be the default photograph for an individual in the People workspace and in reports and charts.

1. Click the **People** button on the main toolbar. Make sure the individual you want to add a portrait to is the focus of the Family tab or Person tab.

2. In the editing panel, right-click the silhouette image and do one of these options.

    •   If the photo you want is already in your tree, click **Link to Existing Picture**. A media item window opens. Click the photo you want and then click **OK**.

    •   If you are adding a new photo, click **Add New Picture**. Use the file management window to navigate to the photo you want. Then click **Open**.

You will now see the photo next to the individual's name in the editing panel. (If you are using a new image, it will automatically be added to your tree; you can view it on the Media workspace.)

Linking a Media Item to Multiple Individuals

You may have a family photo that includes several individuals in your tree. You don't have to add the picture to each individual; simply add it once to the Media workspace and then link it to the necessary individuals. You can also link media items to specific facts. For example, if you have a photograph or drawing of the ship on which your grandparents immigrated to America, you can link the picture to your grandparents and their immigration fact.

1. Go to the **Collection** tab on the Media workspace. In the Media workspace, double-click the item you want to link to multiple individuals, or click the item and then click the **Detail** tab.

2. At the bottom of the Detail tab, you'll see a Links tab. Click the **New** button and choose **Link to Person**.

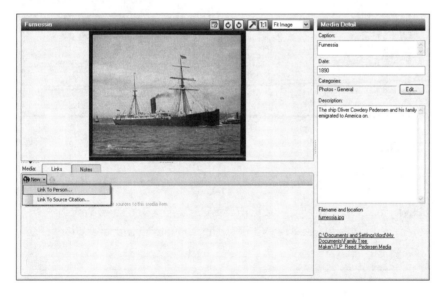

3. In the **Name** column, click the name of the individual you want to link the item to.

4. Do one of these options:

- To link the item to a person, click **Link to person only**. (You can link only one person at a time.)

- To link the item to a specific fact (such as birth or marriage), click **Link to person's fact**. Then click the fact in the list below.

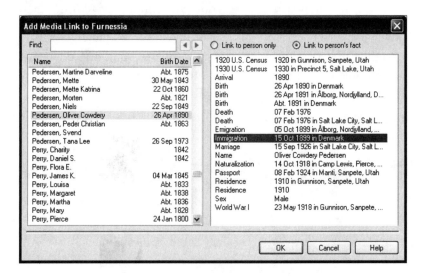

5. Click **OK**.

> **TIP**
>
> If you mistakenly link a media item to an individual, you can unlink the item on the item's Detail tab. Click the appropriate individual and then click the broken link icon.

Managing Media Items

After you've added media items to your tree, you might need to do some maintenance tasks. You can change file names, view and edit items, and assign categories.

Changing the Display of an Image

When you're viewing a photo, you can change the display of the image by rotating the image or zooming in and out on the image.

Go to the **Collection** tab on the Media workspace. Double-click the photo you want to change the display for, or click the image, then click the **Detail** tab.

Use these buttons in the image toolbar to change the display:

Click the **Rotate right** button to move the image in a clockwise direction; click the **Rotate left** button to move the image in a counterclockwise direction.

Click the **Size to fit** button to display the entire image in the current window.

Click the **Actual size** button to show the actual size of the image. You can also choose a specific size percentage from the **Fit Image** drop-down list.

Opening a Media Item from Family Tree Maker

If you need to edit an image or open a document you've added to Family Tree Maker, you can open the media item in its default program without leaving Family Tree Maker. For example, you could open a PDF document in Adobe Reader.

Go to the **Collection** tab on the Media workspace. Double-click the photo you want to change the display for, or click the image, then click the **Detail** tab. Then use this button to open the media item:

 Click the **Open file** button in the image toolbar. The media item opens in the file's default program. If you edit the media item and save your changes, the modified file will be linked to Family Tree Maker.

Changing a Media Item's File Name

Family Tree Maker lets you change a media item's actual file name on your hard drive—from within the software. This can be useful if you've imported a tree and its media files have been copied to your computer with generic names; you can use Family Tree Maker to make their file names more identifiable.

1. Go to the **Collection** tab on the Media workspace. Right-click a media item and choose **Rename Media File** from the drop-down list, or click a media item and choose **Media>Rename Media File**.

2. Enter the new name for the file and click **OK**.

Arranging an Individual's Media Items

When you add media items for an individual, they are arranged in alphabetical order (by caption). If you want, you can change the order in which they appear on the Media tab. For example, you may want to display the pictures by date or age.

1. Go to the **Person** tab on the People workspace and select the appropriate individual.

2. Click the **Media** tab at the bottom of the window. The tab shows thumb-
    nails of any media items you've linked to this individual.

Use these buttons in the media toolbar to change the display order:

 Click the item you want to move. Then click the **Move Media
Forward** and **Move Media Backwards** buttons to rearrange the
media items. The items will remain in the sort you've chosen.

 Click the **Auto Sort Media** button to sort the media items
alphabetically (by caption).

Media Categories

As you add each media item to your tree, you can assign it to categories. These
categories make your media items easier to search for, sort, and view.

Creating a Category

You can use the default categories in Family Tree Maker, modify them, or create your own. If you decide to create your own categories, you might want to
set up a system before you add your media items. For example, you may want
to have event categories (e.g., Weddings, Birthdays, Travel) or categories based
on item types (e.g., Photos—Portraits, Movies—Holidays).

1. Go to the **Collection** tab on the Media workspace. In the media editing
    panel, click the **Edit** button.

2. Click the **Add button**.

3. Enter a name for the category and click **OK**.

Assigning a Category to Multiple Items

Family Tree Maker lets you assign categories to a group of items at the same time.

1. Go to the **Collection** tab on the Media workspace.

2. Select the media items you want to assign a category to. You can select multiple media items by clicking on each file you want while holding down the **CTRL** key.

3. Click **Media>Categorize Media**.

4. From the drop-down list, you can choose each image one by one or all selected images.

5. Click the checkboxes for the categories you want to assign the items to and click **OK**.

Printing a Media Item

1. Go to the **Collection** tab on the Media workspace and click on the item you want to print.

2. Click the **Print** button on the main toolbar and choose **Print Media Item** from the drop-down list.

3. Just like printing from any other application, you can choose a printer, select the number of copies, and choose a page range.

4. Click **Print**.

Creating a Slide Show

You can create a slide show of pictures you've included in your tree—and even include a soundtrack. You can view your completed slide shows using *Windows Media Player*.

1. Click the **Media** button on the main toolbar. Click **Media> Create Slide Show**.

> **TIP**
> You can create a slide show for a specific individual by clicking the **Create slide show** button on the individual's Media tab.

2. Change the slide show options as necessary:

   - **Title.** Enter a name for the slide show. (This will be the item's file name on your computer also.)

   - **Images to include.** If you want to include pictures from a specific category, choose the category name from the drop-down list. Then click the **Include relationship media** checkbox to include images linked to relationships; click the **Include fact media** checkbox to include images linked to facts.

   - **Image caption.** Choose how you want captions displayed in the slide show. Click **None** if you don't want captions displayed; click **Use Captions Only** to display image captions; click **Use Filenames Only** to display file names; click **Use Captions or Filenames** to display captions (or if no caption has been entered, an image's file name will be displayed).

     Click the **Font** button to choose a font style, size, and color for captions and file names used in the slide show.

   - **Movie size.** Choose the display size of the slide show from the drop-down list.

     Note: The larger the movie, the more memory required.

   - **Movie quality.** Choose the display quality of the slide show from the drop-down list.

     Note: The better quality the movie, the more memory required.

   - **Transition delay.** Choose the number of seconds an image is displayed.

   - **Sound track.** If you would like to add music to the slide show, click the **Browse** button and locate the audio file you'd like to use. You can use any MP3 or Windows Media Audio (.wma) file.

3. Click **Next**. A window opens, displaying all the images you've chosen. You can change the order in which images appear or delete images you don't want.

4. Click **Next**. A preview window opens.

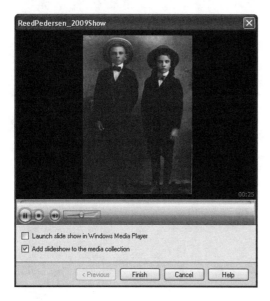

5. Do one of these options:

    • To save the slide show to your tree, click **Add slide show to the media collection**.

    • To view the finished slide show in *Windows Media Player*, click **Launch slide show in Windows Media Player**.

6. Click **Finish**. A message asks whether you want to save the file to your tree or save the file to another location.

7. Click **Save this file to the media folder** to save the slide show to the Family Tree Maker media folder, or click **Save the slide show in another location** to choose a location.

8. Click the checkbox for the category you want this item to belong to; you can select multiple categories.

9. Click **OK**. The item is added to the Media workspace.

Chapter Seven
Using Maps

As you gather the names and dates of important events in your ancestors' lives, you'll also record the locations where these events took place—the homes, towns and cities, states, and countries that shaped their daily lives.

Often, these locations exist only as names in a report or on a pedigree chart. Family Tree Maker brings these ancestral homelands to life by letting you virtually visit each place in your tree. For example, you can see satellite images and maps of the town in Denmark where your grandfather was born, the apartment house in Chicago where your great-grandparents lived, or even the lake where you went swimming with your cousins every summer.

Family Tree Maker gives you the chance to become familiar with lands that you may never be able to visit in real life. See where your family lived, follow their immigration path, or watch their progress as they move from city to city, sometimes across the country.

Each time you enter a place name for a fact or event, Family Tree Maker adds this location to a "master list" of locations. To view this master list, simply go to the Places workspace. You can then view maps and satellite images of a location, identify individuals in your tree who are associated with certain locations, and more.

Viewing a Map

The interactive online maps in Family Tree Maker are easy to navigate using a few simple tools. You can zoom in and out on the map, change the type of map you're viewing, and more.

Note: You must be connected to the Internet to use the online mapping feature.

1. Click the **Places** button on the main toolbar. To access a map, click a location in the **Places** panel.

    Immediately, a road map (the default view) will appear in the display area, the specified location centered on the map and marked with a red pushpin. In the top, left-hand corner of the map you'll notice the Map Tools. These tools remain on the map regardless of which view you're looking at.

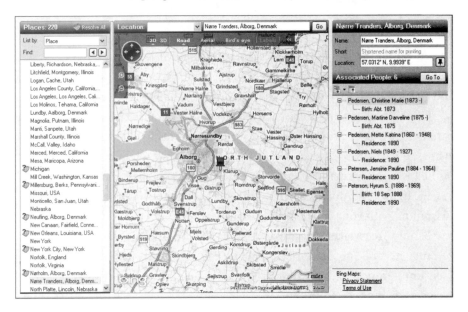

    To change the type of map you're viewing, simply click the appropriate view in the Map Tools.

TIP

You can hide the Map Tools by clicking the arrow button on the far right side of the toolbar. Click the arrow again to display the tools.

---

2. Click **Aerial** to view a satellite image of the location.

3. In the aerial view, you can click **Labels** to switch between the aerial view and a combination of the road view and the aerial view.

4. Click **Road** to display the street map again.

5. To see a street-level view of the location, click **Bird's eye**. Click the points of the compass on the Map Tools to change the direction you are viewing.

Note: At this time, the bird's-eye view is available only for certain parts of the world.

Microsoft® Bing™ Maps

Family Tree Maker has partnered with Microsoft *Bing Maps* to let you access some of the most exciting technology available today. *Bing Maps* takes you beyond typical road maps by combining them with special satellite and aerial imagery to let you experience the world as it looks today.

As you visit different locations, you'll notice that the level of detail that you can see for each town, region, or country varies. In some areas you can zoom in close enough to see cars, rooftops, and street intersections; in other areas your view will disappear when you get within a mile of the location. Fortunately, *Bing Maps* is updated regularly and regions that may not have many images now will in the future. The most detailed views are of the United States, the United Kingdom, Canada, and Australia.

And if you're worried about how these satellite images may affect your privacy, you'll be glad to know that these images are not "live." In addition, you may be able to see details of houses, roads, and trees, but the images are of a low enough resolution that you can't read signs or identify people.

Note: This feature is subject to change without notice.

6. Click **3D** to change the map from two dimensions to three. You can use the 3-D mode in the road and aerial views. (The first time you click the 3D button, you will be prompted to download additional plug-in software from Microsoft. You can't view 3-D maps without this software.)

To rotate the image, press the **CTRL** key on your keyboard and hold down the left mouse button as you move the mouse around. Maneuvering in 3-D can be tricky, so it might take some practice before you're able to view the map exactly as you'd like.

Note: You can also change the 3-D view by clicking the **Rotate camera** and **Tilt** buttons.

Moving Around a Map

If the part of the map that you want to see isn't available in the current view, you can quickly view any adjacent parts of the map by "dragging" it. Move the cursor over the map. When the cursor shape changes to a hand, click and hold down either mouse key. Now drag the map wherever you want.

Zooming In and Out on a Map

You can use the plus and minus buttons on the Map Tools to zoom in and out on the displayed map.

1. Click the plus sign (+) button to magnify the map one level at a time; click the button and hold the mouse button down to rapidly zoom in on the map.

2. Click the minus sign (-) button to minimize the map one level at a time; click the button and hold the mouse button down to rapidly zoom out on the map.

Note: If you try to view an area where satellite imagery is not available, the map will change to a white screen.

Finding Places of Interest

In addition to viewing event locations you've added to your tree, Family Tree Maker lets you search for places of interest such as libraries, cemeteries, and churches. If you're planning a genealogy research trip, you can use Family Tree Maker to view all the cemeteries and churches in your ancestor's hometown. You can also type in other attractions and sites you want to search for—try entering "hotel", "park", or even "gas station".

1. Click the **Places** button on the main toolbar.

2. If you have already entered the location in your tree, click its name in the **Places** panel; otherwise, enter the location's name in the blank field above the map (the one on the right).

3. Choose a location type (such as cemeteries) from the drop-down list and click **Go**. (You can also type in your own search term in the drop-down list.) Blue pushpins will appear for each location that matches your search.

4. Move the mouse over each pushpin to see a name and address for the location (if available).

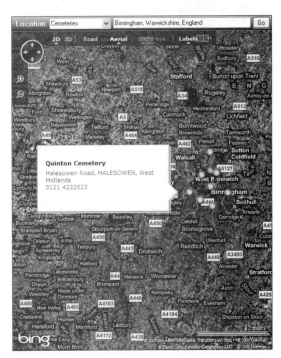

Printing a Map

Family Tree Maker lets you print maps directly from the software, whether it's an aerial shot of your ancestor's farm or the migration path your great-grandfather took across the country.

Note: You can print two- and three-dimensional maps, but not bird's-eye views.

1. On the Places workspace, access the map you want to print. Because the map will print as it is shown in the display window, you may want to resize the workspace to display more of the map.

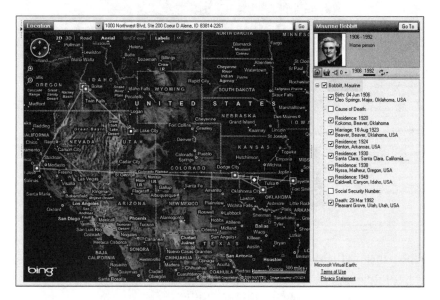

2. In the map toolbar, click the **Print** button and choose **Print Map** from the drop-down list. The Print window opens.

    Just like printing from any other application, you can choose a printer, select the number of copies to print, and more.

3. Click **OK**.

Viewing Facts Associated with a Location

When you enter a fact for an individual, you have the option to also enter the location where the event occurred. Family Tree Maker lets you view all the events that took place at a certain location—and view the people who are associated with each event.

1. Click the **Places** button on the main toolbar.

2. Click a location in the **Places** panel.

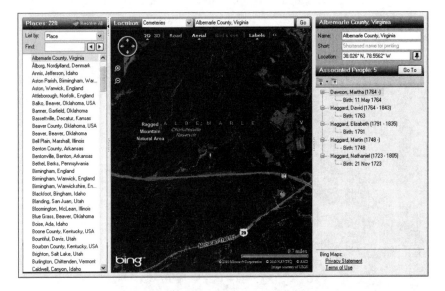

In the panel on the right side of the window, you'll now see the name of the location and underneath it, a list of names. The individuals in the list all have life events associated with the location.

3. Do one of these options:

   - If you want to see the event that occurred at this location for a specific individual, click the plus sign (+) next to the individual's name.

   - If you want to see the events that occurred at this location for all the individuals, click the **Expand all items** button on the toolbar and choose **Expand all**. (Click the **Collapse all items** button to close all the events.)

- If you want location events to always appear in the panel, click the **Expand all items** button on the toolbar and choose **Expand All on Load.**

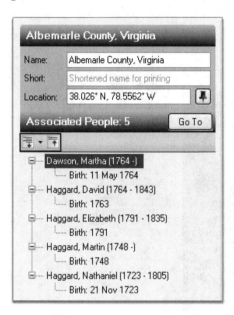

Note: You can click the **Go To** button to access the highlighted event or individual in the People workspace.

Viewing Migration Maps

Maps can be one of the most useful family history resources you'll use when tracing an ancestor. Family Tree Maker lets you see at a glance all the locations that are connected with a specific individual or family. You can view locations important to an individual, track migration patterns, and maybe discover where to locate more records.

Viewing a Migration Map for an Individual

1. Click the **Places** button on the main toolbar. In the panel on the left side of the window, choose "Person" from the **List by** drop-down list.

2. Click the name of the individual whose locations you want to see. A
   labeled aerial map will appear in the display area; the individual's birthplace is indicated by a green marker, and the individual's death place is
   indicated by a red marker. To the right of the map is a list of every fact
   you've entered for an individual—and its location.

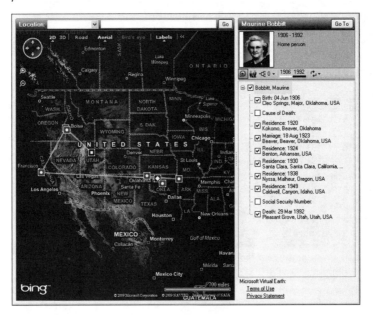

3. Click the checkbox next to a fact to include the location of that event on
   the map.

4. Move the mouse over each marker to see the location's name and the fact
   associated with it.

Maps and Family History

While maps are often sought for their visual appeal, they also can offer clues to locating records and information about your family. Using a variety of geographic resources, you can follow your ancestors' lives as they move from city to city, state to state, and sometimes country to country. Maps can also help you learn where local record repositories, courthouses, and cemeteries are located. Here are some examples of different resources you might want to locate:

- **Atlases.** Contain groups of maps for states, cities, and more.
- **Gazetteers or geographical dictionaries.** In addition to place names, these include information about various land features such as mountains, lakes and rivers, and sometimes even cemeteries.
- **Road maps.** Show roads, highways, railroads, cities, and more.
- **Topographical maps.** Show land features, including hills, mountains, and bodies of water.
- **Political maps.** Show boundaries for states, counties, cities.

You should locate maps that show the land as it existed when your ancestors lived there. Because state, county, and city boundaries change over time, the more historically accurate the map is, the more useful it will be.

Viewing a Migration Map for a Family

1. Click the **Places** button on the main toolbar. In the **Places** panel, choose "Person" from the **List by** drop-down and click the name of an individual.

2. To view the locations associated with the individual's immediate family (parents, siblings, spouse, and children), click the **Include immediate family** button in the mapping toolbar.

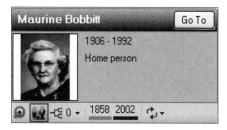

3. Click an individual's name to the right of the map to highlight his or her life events on the map. The migration path for the individual is indicated by a thick line.

> ### TIP
> You can change the color of a migration path by clicking the line color buttons in the mapping toolbar.

4. To view locations associated with an individual's ancestors (up to four generations), click the **Ancestor generations** button in the mapping toolbar and choose the number of generations from the drop-down list.

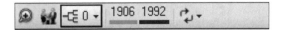

A labeled map will appear in the display area: birthplaces are indicated by green markers, and death places are indicated by red markers; the migration path for each individual is indicated by a colored line.

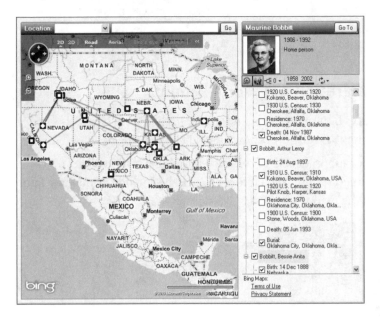

Entering GPS Coordinates for a Location

Although the online mapping feature is able to recognize millions of locations, there are times when it won't be able to identify the exact location of a place you've entered. Perhaps your relatives are buried in a rural cemetery that doesn't appear on the map. Or perhaps census records show that your family lived in a township that no longer exists. You can set the exact position for the location using GPS (Global Positioning System) coordinates.

1. Click the **Places** button on the main toolbar. In the **Places** panel, click the name of the location to which you want to add GPS coordinates.

2. Place your cursor in the **Location** field and click the **Location calculator** icon that appears.

The Location Calculator window opens. You can enter the coordinates in degrees:minutes:seconds, degrees:decimal minutes, or decimal degrees.

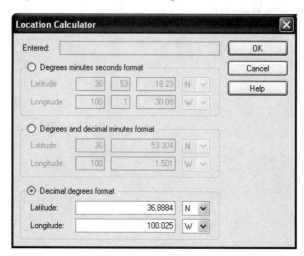

3. Enter the coordinates for the location and click **OK**.

Entering a Display Name for a Location

Recording locations in a complete and consistent manner is an important part of creating a quality family history. Unfortunately, those long location names can become unwieldy and clutter your reports and charts. Family Tree Maker lets you enter your own shortened or abbreviated display names that can be used for charts and reports. For example, instead of a birthplace being listed as Heidelberg, Baden-Württemberg, Germany, you can enter Heidelberg, Germany, as the display name.

1. Click the **Places** button on the main toolbar.
2. In the **Places** panel, choose "Place" from the **List by** drop-down list.
3. Click the name of the location you want to change.
4. In the **Short** field enter a display name.

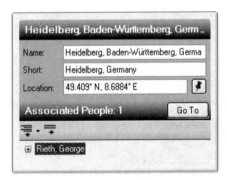

Chapter Eight
Researching Your Tree Online

As you enter family stories and facts into Family Tree Maker, you will probably notice that more information about your family is waiting to be discovered—perhaps it's the burial location of your grandfather or the wedding certificate for your aunt and uncle. Family Tree Maker can help you fill in these gaps in your research. When you connect to the Internet, Family Tree Maker can automatically perform behind-the-scenes searches of Ancestry.com and alert you when it has found information that might match individuals in your tree.

You can also use Family Tree Maker to search the vast number of family history resources available on the Web. Search for information on RootsWeb.com, Genealogy.com, or any of your favorite websites. And if you find information that matches a family member, you can quickly add it to your tree—all without leaving Family Tree Maker.

Ancestry Hints

Family Tree Maker automatically searches the thousands of databases on Ancestry.com—census records; birth, marriage, and death records; court and land records; immigration records; military records; family trees; and more—looking for information that matches people in your tree. When a possible match is found, a green leaf or "hint" appears next to an individual's name in the pedigree view and editing panel on the People workspace (fig. 8-1).

Figure 8-1

A leaf on the editing panel shows that the individual has Ancestry hints waiting to be viewed.

You can view the results when it's convenient, and if the information is relevant, you can merge it into your tree.

Note: If you don't want Family Tree Maker to automatically search Ancestry.com when you are connected to the Internet, you can turn this feature off. You can also exclude Ancestry Member Trees from hints. To change these preferences, click **Tools>Options**.

Viewing Hints

If Family Tree Maker finds records or trees on Ancestry.com that possibly match an individual in your tree, you'll see a green leaf next to the individual's name on the People workspace. To view these hints, simply move the mouse over the leaf icon and you'll see the number of records and trees that were found on Ancestry.com.

To view the actual records and trees on Ancestry.com, simply click the leaf. The Web Search workspace opens and displays the search results. If you find a record that matches the individual, you can quickly merge the results into your tree. If a search result doesn't match anyone in your tree, you can choose to ignore it—it will no longer show up on Ancestry hints.

Note: To view Ancestry hint search results on Ancestry.com, you must register your copy of Family Tree Maker and have an Internet connection. To view the actual records, you must have a subscription to Ancestry.com.

1. Go to the **Family** tab on the People workspace. In the pedigree view or editing panel, move the mouse over the leaf icon. You will see the number of records and trees that possibly match the selected individual.

2. Click the **Ancestry hints found** link. The Web Search workspace opens. In the browser you can see the Ancestry.com search results that are possible matches for the selected individual. You may need to scroll down the window to see all available results.

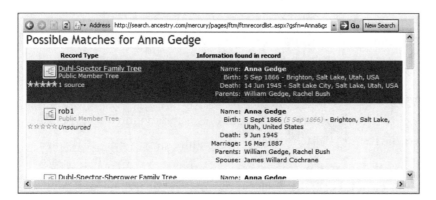

3. Click on any search results that interest you. If the record matches someone in your family, you can merge the information into your tree. (For instructions, see "Merging Ancestry.com Records into a Tree" on page 118.) If the record does not match anyone in your tree, you can choose to ignore the record. (For instructions, see the next task, "Ignoring Hints".)

Ignoring Hints

If a hint you've accessed is not relevant to anyone in your tree, you can choose to ignore it. That way the record won't show up in Ancestry hints again.

1. Access the Ancestry hints for an individual. On the Possible Matches page, click the search result that you want to ignore.

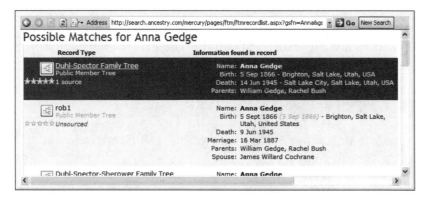

2. On the Search Result Detail toolbar, click the **Ignore record** button (a circle with a diagonal line through it).

The Ignore record button changes to yellow to show that the record is being ignored. When you return to the Person workspace this record will not appear in Ancestry hints.

Viewing Ignored Hints

If you've chosen to ignore specific Ancestry hints for an individual, you can still access the results at a later time.

1. Click the **Web Search** button on the main toolbar. Using the mini pedigree tree or Index of Individuals button, choose the individual whose hints you'd like to view.

2. Click **Search>View Ignored Records**. (If this individual has no ignored records, a message appears; click **OK** and choose another individual.)

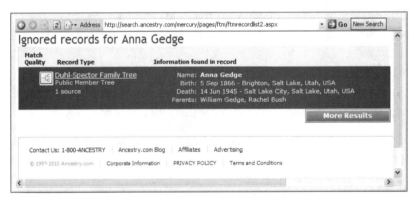

3. If you want to take the search result off the Ignore list, click the **Ignore record** button (a circle with a diagonal line through it).

The Ignore record button changes back to blue. This record will be included in Ancestry hints again.

What Can I Find on Ancestry.com?

Ancestry.com is the world's largest online resource for family history records and family trees. It has thousands of unique databases, with more being added all the time. If you don't find what you're looking for today, try again in a few weeks. Here's a sample of the wealth of resources available on Ancestry:

- The world's only complete U.S. census collection (1790–1930). You'll also find census records for Canada and the UK.
- The largest online collection of immigration records, with passenger lists from 1820 to 1960.
- More than 50 million African American records, including slave narratives, censuses, and U.S. Colored Troops service records.
- Birth, marriage, and death records.
- More than 100 million military records covering the 1600s through Vietnam.
- Historical newspapers spanning the 1700s through 2003.
- More than 20,000 books—local histories, memoirs, journals, biographies, and more.
- Court, land, and probate records.
- Thousands of photos from the Library of Congress, maps beginning in the 1500s, historical photographs dating back to the mid-1800s, land ownership maps, and millions of photos uploaded by Ancestry members.
- Almost 17 million family trees from all over the world—created by researchers just like you.

Searching Ancestry.com

You don't have to wait for Ancestry hints to help you locate records for your family. Family Tree Maker connects directly to Ancestry.com so you can search the millions of available records at any time.

Note: Although anyone can view Ancestry.com search results, you must have a subscription to access the actual records and images.

1. Click the **Web Search** button on the main toolbar.

2. Click "Ancestry.com" in the Search Locations list. If you want to research a different individual than the one who is currently selected, use the mini pedigree tree or Index of Individuals button to choose the appropriate person.

   In the browser you'll notice that the search fields have already been filled in with the selected individual's information.

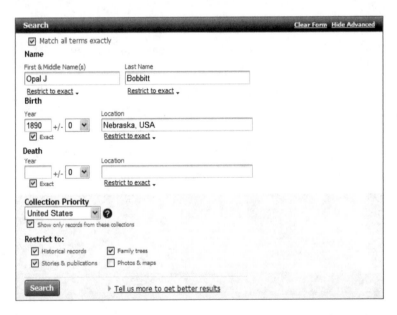

By each field you'll see an Exact checkbox. You can use this option to limit your searches to records that match your search terms exactly. To get the most out of an exact search, you should start by only entering one or two search terms, such as name and location.

3. Add or delete names, dates, and places as necessary.

4. If you want records relating to a specific country or ethnicity listed first in your search results, choose an option from the **Collection Priority** drop-down list.

5. If you want you can limit your search results to a specific type of record:

   • Click the **Historical Records** checkbox to search for census records, military and immigration records, birth records, etc.

   • Click the **Stories and Publications** checkbox to search for member-submitted stories, newspapers, county histories, etc.

   • Click the **Family Trees** checkbox to search trees submitted by members.

   • Click the **Photos and maps** checkbox to search maps, postcards, photo collections, member-submitted photos, etc.

6. After making your selections, click **Search**. A page of search results appears. On the left side of the page you'll see your search terms. On the right side you'll see the different records located on Ancestry that might match your family member. Notice that each match has a rating—the greater the number of stars, the better the match will be.

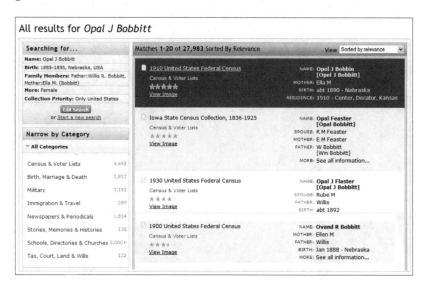

Search Tips

When you search records at Ancestry, it puts the best matches at the top of the list. Ancestry also includes name variations, abbreviations, and nicknames in a search. But if you're searching for an elusive ancestor, you may need some additional assistance. Here are some tips to help you get the most out of your searches:

- **Use wildcards.** Wildcards are special symbols used to represent unknown letters in a word. You can use an asterisk for up to six characters. For example, a search for "fran*" will return matches such as Fran, Franny, Frank, Frannie, and Frankie. Use a question mark for a single character. For example, a search for "Hans?n" will return matches such as Hansen and Hanson.

- **Search for similar-sounding names.** If you are using the "Exact matches" option, you can search for last names that "sound like" the one you're looking for. For example, a search for Smith would return Smithe, Smyth, and Smythe. To use this type of search, click the "Restrict to exact" link under the individual's surname. Then click the **Soundex** and **Phonetic** checkboxes.

- **Estimate dates.** If you're not sure of the exact date of an event, make an educated guess. You'll get much better results than if you leave the field blank.

- **Narrow your search.** Try searching a specific type of record, such as a census, or a specific database, such as World War II draft registration records.

- **Add multiple locations.** If your family member lived in New York, Pennsylvania, and Illinois, add each of these residences to your search and you'll get search results for all locations at once. To do this, click the "Tell us more link'" at the bottom of the search page. Then add additional locations in the "Lived In" fields.

7. If you get a large number of search results or matches, you can add more information to narrow your search. Try adding more dates, a spouse's name, gender, or race. (You can also narrow your search by clicking a category link on the left side of the window.) If you get too few results or no matches, delete one or more of your search terms to broaden your search.

8. Click a search result to see the record or index. The tab at the bottom of the window lets you compare, side-by-side, the facts in your tree with the details found in the highlighted Ancestry record.

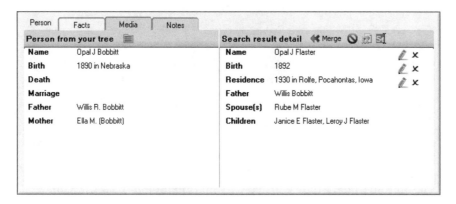

9. If the information matches what you already know about the individual and his or her family, you can merge the information into your tree. (For instructions, see the next task, "Merging Ancestry.com Records into a Tree.")

Merging Ancestry.com Records into a Tree

Once you identify a relevant record or family tree on Ancestry.com, you can merge the information directly into your tree using the Web Merge Wizard. You can choose the pieces of information you wish to incorporate and whether that information should become "preferred" or "alternate" information. It will even include record images and source information for you automatically.

Note: The Web Merge process does not overwrite any of the data in your tree. However, it is always a good idea to save a backup of your file before making major changes.

1. In the Web Search workspace, access the Ancestry.com record or tree that you want to merge into your tree.

2. Make sure the individual you want to merge the record to is selected in the Person from Your Tree section. If you need to merge the record with a different person, click the **Select a Different Person** button (a file folder icon) in the toolbar. Choose an individual and click **OK**.

The bottom of the window displays the information in your tree compared side-by-side with the information found in the Ancestry record.

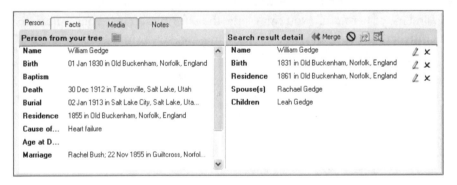

3. Click **Merge**. The Web Merge Wizard will launch. Depending on the type of record you're accessing, the wizard may contain multiple pages.

The left side of the window lists the names of all the people included in the record you are merging. As you move through the wizard, each individual will be highlighted as you make decisions about his or her information. Next to the individuals' names, you'll see three columns: the Person from My Tree column shows the information you already have in your tree; the Person from Web Search column shows the information from the record and lets you choose how to handle the information (i.e., ignore, make preferred, make alternate); and the Merged Result column shows how the information will be added to your tree.

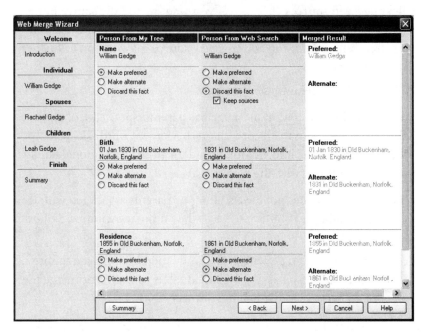

4. In the Person from Web Search column, choose how you want the information found on Ancestry.com to be merged into your tree:

- **Make preferred.** Enter the new information as the "preferred" fact for the individual.

- **Make alternate.** Enter the new information as an alternate fact for the individual.

- **Discard this fact.** Do not merge the new information into your tree. (You may choose to ignore some facts from a record, although it is usually a good idea to include all facts from a particular record in case they turn out to be relevant.)

   Click the **Keep sources** checkbox if you want to add the source but not the fact. For example, you may already have a birth date listed in your tree, but you want to add this new source information to further validate the fact.

5. Click **Next** and do one of these options:

- If the individual you want to merge has parents, spouse(s), or children associated with the record, the Web Merge Wizard asks you if you want to add the information found for the first additional family member. Continue with the next step.

- If the individual does not have siblings or parents associated with this source, click the **Next** button to go to the Summary window. Skip to step 8.

6. Choose what you want to do with each family member. You can ignore the person, add the person as a new individual in your tree, or merge the person with an existing individual in your tree.

   The details about the additional family members appear in the Person from Web Search column, while the information you already have in your tree appears in the Person from My Tree column. You can compare the information you have with what Family Tree Maker has found on Ancestry.com. If more than one individual appears in the Person from My Tree column, you will need to select the individual with whom you want to merge the new information.

7. Click **Next** and complete step 6 for every name in the record until all additional family members have been looked through. When you have made decisions for each family member, the Summary window opens.

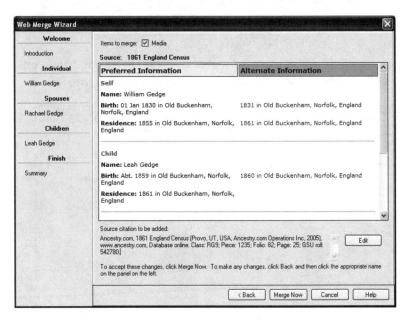

8. Verify your selections in the Summary window. If you want to include an image of a record as a media item, click the **Media** checkbox. When you're ready, click **Merge Now**. A message tells you when the Web Search result has been successfully merged into your tree. Click **OK** to close the message.

Note: You *cannot* undo a merge. However, none of your existing information will be overwritten, so if you decide you made a mistake, you can simply delete the fact(s) or source(s) that you added during the merge.

Searching Online with Family Tree Maker

With Family Tree Maker, you have a convenient starting point for researching and expanding your family history—without interrupting your work. You can explore the Web using any of your favorite search engines or genealogy websites. Although Family Tree Maker won't automatically search websites other than Ancestry.com, it does provide a "Web clipping" tool that lets you select text and images you're interested in and add it to individuals in your tree.

1. Click the **Web Search** button on the main toolbar. Using the mini pedigree tree or Index of Individuals button, choose the individual whose information you want to search for.

2. In **Search Locations**, click the website that you want to search, or enter a website in the **Address** field of the Web browser. The website opens.

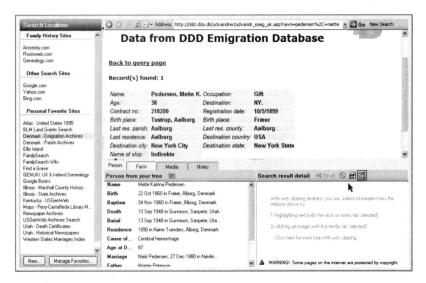

3. Look for information on your ancestors just as you would if you were performing any kind of online search.

Copying Online Facts

If you find family facts such as a birth date or birthplace on a website that you'd like to add to your tree, you can use the Family Tree Maker "Web clipping" tool to select the information. In some cases, Family Tree Maker will recognize the type of information you're trying to add and will give you relevant fields to choose from. For example, if you try to add information from the Social Security Death Index, you'll have the option to add the selected text to a name, Social Security Number, birth fact, death fact, or Social Security Issued fact.

1. Access the website you want to copy facts from.

2. If you want to link the facts to a person in your tree who is different from the currently selected individual, click the **Select a different person** button in the Person from Your Tree section. Choose an individual and click **OK**.

3. Click the **Facts** tab at the bottom of the window. On the Search Result Detail toolbar, click the **Enable web clipping** button. (You can tell when Web clipping is enabled because the icon has a yellow box around it.)

4. Move the mouse over text on the website until the pointer turns into a cursor. Highlight the text you want to copy. A drop-down list appears.

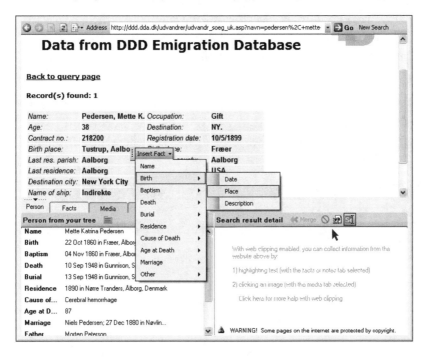

5. Choose a fact from the **Insert Fact** drop-down list. For example, you can choose the birthplace fact. The highlighted information now appears in the Search Result Detail section.

Note: You can add multiple facts to your tree before merging the information; you don't need to merge each fact separately.

6. When you have selected all the information you want, click **Merge**. The Web Merge Wizard will launch.

7. In the Person from Web Search column, choose how you want the information to be merged into your tree:

   • **Make preferred.** Enter the new information as the "preferred" fact for the individual.

   • **Make alternate.** Enter the new information as an alternate fact for the individual.

   • **Discard this fact.** Do not merge the new information into your tree. Click the **Keep sources** checkbox if you want to keep the new source information (the URL where the information was located) but not the fact. (You can also enter source information on the Summary page.)

8. Click **Summary** to see how the information will be added to your tree. If necessary, click **Edit** to enter a source citation for the information. (The default source citation is the URL, or Web address, where the information was located.)

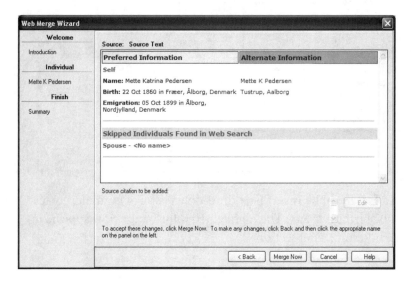

9. Click **Merge Now**. A message tells you when the online facts have been successfully merged into your tree. Click **OK** to close the message.

Copying an Online Image

You may find family photos or images of historical documents online that will enhance the family history you're compiling. Family Tree Maker makes it easy to add these directly from a website to your tree.

> Note: Before downloading any images from the Web, make sure you aren't violating any copyright restrictions and/or get permission from the owner.

1. Access the online image you want.

2. If you want to link the image to a person in your tree who is different from the currently selected individual, click the **Select a different person** button in the Person from Your Tree section. Choose an individual and click **OK**.

3. Click the **Media** tab at the bottom of the window. On the Search Result Detail toolbar, click the **Enable web clipping** button. (You can tell when Web clipping is enabled because the icon has a yellow box around it.)

4. Move the mouse over the Web page until the image you want is highlighted by a green dotted line.

5. Click the highlighted image. A thumbnail of the image appears in the Search Result Detail section.

6. When you have selected all the images you want, click **Merge**. A message tells you when the image has been successfully merged into your tree. Click **OK** to close the message.

Note: The image will be linked to the person displayed in the "Person from Your Tree" section. You can now view the item on the Media workspace. If you want to link the image to a different person in your tree, see "Linking a Media Item to Multiple Individuals" on page 83.

Copying Online Text to a Note

While you're looking online for information about your family, you may come upon interesting stories about the founding of your grandfather's hometown or a description of the ship your great-grandparents sailed to America on. Or you might find clues that will help you further your research goals. You can easily preserve this type of information using the "Web clipping" tool.

1. Access the website you want to copy information from.

2. If you want to link the notes to a person in your tree who is different from the currently selected individual, click the **Select a different person** button in the Person from Your Tree section. Choose an individual and click **OK**.

3. Click the **Notes** tab at the bottom of the window. If you want to add the information as a personal note, click the **Person note** button on the toolbar. If you want to add the information as a research note, click the **Research note** button on the toolbar.

4. On the Search Result Detail toolbar, click the **Enable web clipping** button.

5. Move the mouse over text on the website until the pointer turns into a cursor. Highlight the text you want to copy. The Insert note button appears.

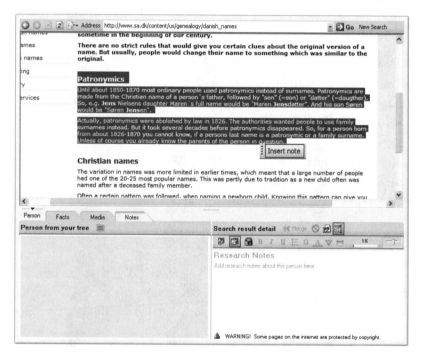

6. Click **Insert note**. The information now appears in the Search Result Detail section.

7. Click **Merge**. A message tells you when the note has been successfully merged into your tree. Click **OK** to close the message.

Note: The notes will be linked to the person displayed in the Person from Your Tree section. To view the notes later, go to the individual's Person tab on the People workspace. Then click the Notes tab at the bottom of the window.

Archiving a Web Page

Websites are constantly changing and even disappearing. If you find a website you want to refer to multiple times, or if you find a site that contains too much information to read in one sitting, you might want to archive the Web page. That way, you can read the page's contents and continue your research when it's convenient for you—without being connected to the Internet. When you archive a Web page, Family Tree Maker will save a "snapshot" of the page in HTML format that can be opened in any Web browser.

1. Access the Web page you want to archive.

2. If you want to link the archived page to a person in your tree who is different from the currently selected individual, click the **Select a different person** button in the Person from Your Tree section. Choose an individual and click **OK**.

3. Click the **Facts**, **Media**, or **Notes** tab. In the Search Result Detail toolbar, click the **Create page archive** button (a picture frame icon). A thumbnail of the page appears in the Search Result Detail section.

4. Click **Merge**. A message tells you when the archived Web page has been successfully merged into your tree. Click **OK** to close the message. A link to the page now appears in the Person from Your Tree section.

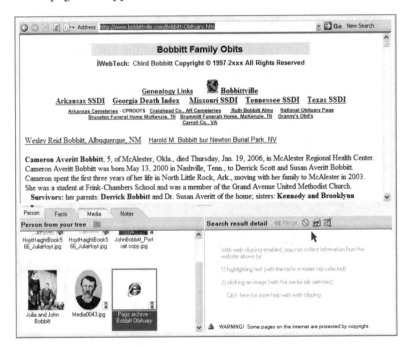

Note: The archived page will be linked to the person displayed in the
Person from Your Tree section. To view the archived page, click the
Media button on the main toolbar to access it on the Media workspace.

Managing Research Websites

As you discover websites that contain valuable information for your family tree,
you'll want to add them to your list of favorite websites so they're easy to visit
again. Websites you add will appear in your favorites list on the left side of the
Web Search workspace under the Personal Favorite Sites heading (fig. 8-2).

Figure 8-2

Websites that have
been added as
favorites.

Adding a Website to Your Favorites List

1. Click the **Web Search** button on the main toolbar. In **Search Locations**,
   click the **New** button.

2. If you are currently accessing the website, click **Use Current Site**. If not, enter the address for the website in the **URL address** field. For example, for the Kentucky GenWeb site, you would enter "www.kygenweb.net".

3. Enter a name for the website in the **Favorite name** field. This can be any name that helps you identify the website.

4. Click **OK**. The new website now appears in your list of personal favorites.

Sorting Your Website Favorites List

After you've gathered quite a few favorite sites, you can sort the list so it appears in an order that's useful to you. For example, if you visit certain websites daily, you may want to put these websites at the top of the list.

1. Click the **Web Search** button on the main toolbar. Click **Manage Favorites**.

2. To display the websites in alphabetical order, click **Sort favorites alphabetically**. To choose your own display order for the websites, click a website in the "Personal favorites list" and then click the up and down arrows. When you're finished, click **OK**.

Part Three

Creating Charts, Reports, and Books

Chapter Nine
Creating Family Tree Charts

After spending time gathering, compiling, and entering your family's history, it's time to reward yourself, show off your hard work, and bring your family history to life. Family Tree Maker offers a wide variety of family tree charts to help you. Add your own personal touch by customizing the charts with attractive backgrounds, colors, photos, fonts, and more. These charts help you quickly view the relationships between family members and are also a fun way to share your discoveries—hang a framed family tree in your home, print out multiple copies to share at a family reunion, or e-mail customized charts to distant relatives.

As you begin creating your own charts, you might want to experiment with various formatting options, print out different versions, and see what you like best.

Pedigree Charts

The pedigree chart is the standard tool of genealogists and what most people think of when they hear the term "family tree." This type of chart shows the direct ancestors of one individual—parents, grandparents, great-grandparents, and so on.

Standard Pedigree Charts

In the standard pedigree chart (fig. 9-1), the primary individual is on the left side of the tree, with ancestors branching off to the right—paternal ancestors on top and maternal ancestors on bottom.

Figure 9-1

A pedigree chart using a custom template.

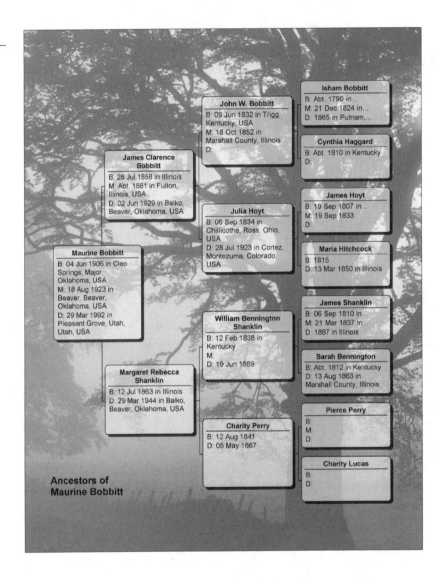

Vertical Pedigree Charts

In the vertical pedigree chart (fig. 9-2), the primary individual is shown at the bottom of the page, with his or her ancestors branching above the individual—paternal ancestors on the left and maternal ancestors on the right.

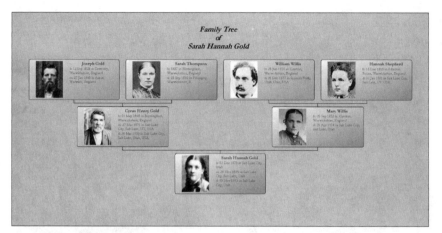

Figure 9-2

A customized vertical pedigree chart with images.

Hourglass Charts

An hourglass chart shows both the ancestors and descendants of a specific individual. The individual appears in the middle of the chart, with ancestors branching off in a shape similar to an hourglass.

> Note: Because of its shape and the number of individuals included, most hourglass charts will look best as posters.

Standard Hourglass Charts

In the standard hourglass chart, the primary individual appears in the middle of the chart, with ancestors branching above and descendants extending below the person.

The chart in figure 9-3 shows an hourglass chart laid out as a poster. Notice the white spaces running vertically and horizontally across the pages. These show the margins of a standard 8½" by 11" sheet of paper. If you want to print the tree at home, you can use these guides to tape the pages together.

You can also create standard hourglass charts that are useful for including in family history books. When you use the book layout, the chart is condensed into a series of individual family trees that appear on separate pages. The chart in figure 9-4 shows one page of a multi-page book-layout chart. Notice the numbered box at the bottom right of the chart. When you are viewing the chart in Family Tree Maker, you can click one of these boxes to access that page of the chart. And when your chart is printed out, the numbered boxes help you navigate to related individuals found on other pages in the chart.

Figure 9-3

An hourglass poster spread over six pages.

Figure 9-4

One page of a standard hourglass book chart.

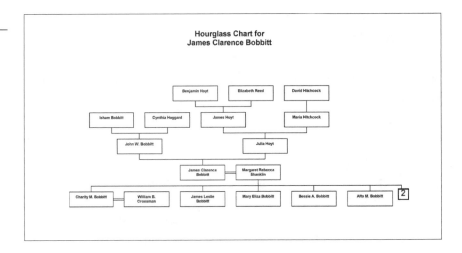

Horizontal Hourglass Charts

In the horizontal hourglass chart (fig. 9-5), the primary individual appears in the middle of the chart with ancestors branching to the right and descendants extending to the left of the person.

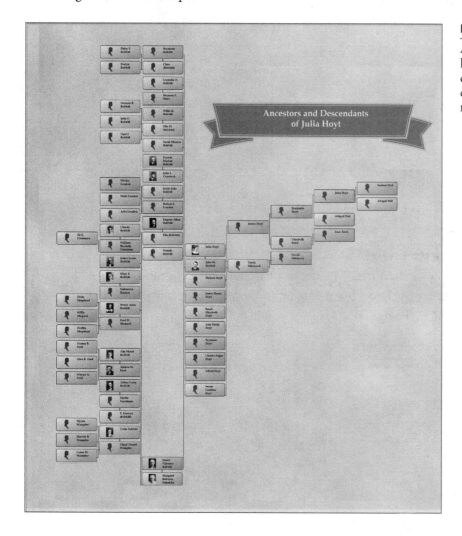

Figure 9-5

A horizontal hourglass chart with embellishments.

Descendant Charts

The descendant chart (fig. 9-6) shows the direct descendants of an individual—children, grandchildren, great-grandchildren, and so on. The primary individual is shown at the top of the chart, with descendants underneath in horizontal rows.

Figure 9-6

A descendant chart with the default settings.

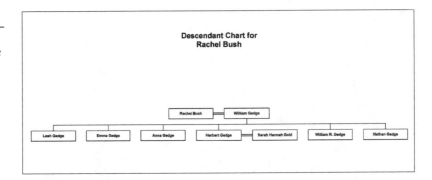

Bow Tie Charts

In the bow tie chart (fig. 9-7), the primary individual appears in the middle with paternal ancestors branching off to the left and maternal ancestors branching to the right.

Figure 9-7

A customized bow tie chart.

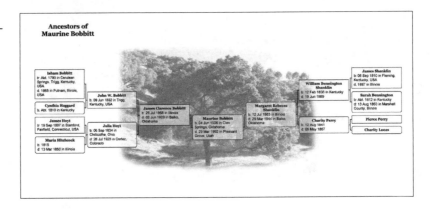

Fan Charts

A fan chart displays an individual's ancestors in a circular shape, one generation per level. The primary individual is at the center or bottom of the chart. You can choose between a full circle, semi-circle, quarter-circle (fig. 9-8), and more.

Note: Because of its shape and the number of individuals included, this chart is available only in poster layout.

Figure 9-8

A customized quarter-circle fan chart.

Family Tree Charts

In the family tree chart (fig. 9-9), the primary individual appears at the bottom of the chart, with ancestors branching above him or her in a tree shape.

Figure 9-9

A customized family tree chart with images.

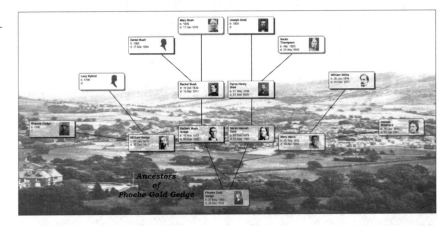

Figure 9-9

A customized family tree chart with images.

Extended Family Charts

The extended family chart (fig. 9-10) can display every individual you've entered in your tree or just the people you select. The chart is arranged so that each generation appears on a separate horizontal row: children, parents, and grandparents, etc.

Note: Because of its shape and the number of individuals included, this chart is available only in poster layout.

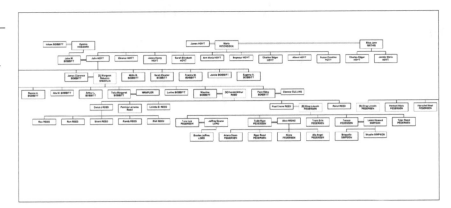

Figure 9-10

A section of a default extended family chart.

Relationship Charts

The relationship chart (fig. 9-11) is a graphical representation of one person's relationship to another—including the relationship of each person in between. The common relative is shown at the top of the chart, with direct-line ancestors and descendants shown vertically beneath the individual.

Figure 9-11

A relationship chart with a patterned background.

Creating a Chart

All charts are based on the last individual you were viewing in your tree. To change the primary individual in the chart, click his or her name in the mini pedigree tree above the chart, or click the Index of Individuals button and choose the person you want.

1. Go to the **Collection** tab on the Publish workspace. In **Publication Types**, click "Charts."

2. Double-click the chart icon, or select its icon and then click the **Detail** tab.

3. Use the editing panel to change the chart.

Customizing a Chart

You can customize the contents and format of charts. For example, you can determine which individuals and facts are included in the chart and choose background images and text options.

Note: Once you've customized a chart, you can save your changes as a template so you can use the same settings again. For instructions, see "Creating Your Own Template" on page 155.

Choosing Facts to Include in a Chart

When customizing a chart, you can often choose which events or facts you'd like to include. Keep in mind, the more facts you include, the larger your tree will be.

1. Access the chart you want to change. In the editing toolbar, click the **Items to include** button.

The Items to Include window opens. The default facts for the chart are shown in the Included facts list. You can add and delete facts for a chart and also change display options for each fact. For example, you can change the order in which a fact displays.

2. Do one of these options:

   • To delete a fact from a chart, click the fact in the Included facts list and click the red (**X**) button.

   • To add a fact to the chart, click the blue (+) button. The Select Fact window opens. Choose a fact from the list and click **OK**.

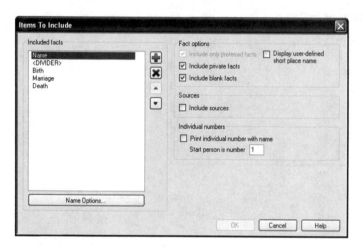

3. Click the **Print individual number with name** checkbox to have Family Tree Maker assign numbers to individuals included in the chart.

4. Choose which types of facts to include or exclude:

   • You may have multiple facts for the same event. Click **Include only preferred facts** to include only the facts designated as "preferred."

   • Click **Include private facts** to include facts designated as "private."

   • Click **Include blank facts** to include a fact field even if the fact has not been entered for an individual.

   • If you have entered shortened place names for locations, click **Display user-defined short place name** to use these locations in the chart.

5. To determine a fact's format in the chart, click the fact in the "Included facts" list and click the **Options** button. Then select the options you want and click **OK**.

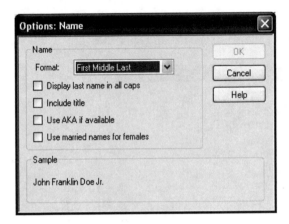

Note: The options for each fact vary. For example, with births, marriages, and deaths, you can include dates and locations.

6. Click **OK** again.

Choosing Individuals to Include in a Chart

The type of chart you create determines which individuals are included in the chart. However, some charts let you include siblings and spouses.

1. Access the chart you want to change. You can choose individuals for the chart in the editing panel.

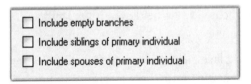

2. To display empty boxes for individuals for whom you've entered no information, click **Include empty branches**.

3. To display the brothers and sisters of the primary individual in the chart, click **Include siblings of primary individual**.

4. To display the spouse(s) of the primary individual, click **Include spouses of primary individual**.

5. You can also choose the number of generations of ancestors (and/or descendants) to display in a chart. To do this, click the **Generations** up and down arrows to choose the number of generations you want to include.

Changing a Chart's Title

You can edit the title that appears at the top of a chart. Access the chart you want to change. In the editing panel, enter a name for the chart in the **Chart title** field.

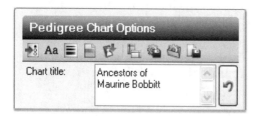

Including Source Information with a Chart

You can include source information with a family tree chart. Sources are not displayed in the actual tree; each sourced fact has a number next to it that corresponds to a list of sources found at the bottom of the chart (fig. 9-12).

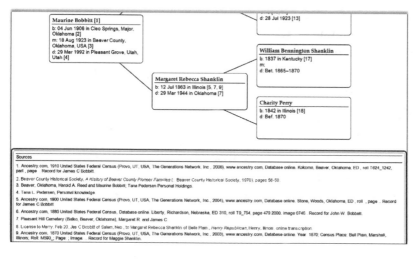

Figure 9-12

Sources on a pedigree chart.

1. Access the chart you want to change. In the editing toolbar, click the **Items to include** button.

2. Click the **Include sources** checkbox. Then click **OK**.

Adding Images to a Chart

You can personalize your charts and make them more appealing by adding backgrounds, family photographs, or individual portraits.

Adding a Background Image

Family Tree Maker comes with several background templates—attractive images you can use as your chart's background. Or you can choose backgrounds from your own images stored on your computer or family pictures you've already added to your tree.

1. Access the chart you want to change. In the **Background** field in the editing panel, choose an image from the drop-down list:

   • To look for an item on your computer's hard drive, click **Browse for Image**. The Select Chart Background Image window opens. Choose an image and click **Open**.

   • To choose an image you've already added to your tree, click **Select from Media Collection**. The Find Media Item window opens. Choose an image and click **OK**.

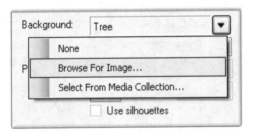

2. Choose how the background will be displayed on the chart. If you want the image centered in the background, choose **Center**. If you want the image stretched to fit the entire page, choose **Stretch**. If you want a close-up

of the image, choose **Zoom**. If you want a series of the same image to fill the background, choose **Tile**.

3. In the **Transparent** drop-down list, choose the intensity of the image. At 0 percent, the image will appear as it normally does, while a higher percentage will fade the image so the chart is easier to read.

Adding Portraits to a Chart

You can include images of individuals in a chart. In order to do this, you must have already added the images to your tree and linked them to specific individuals. (For instructions, see "Assigning a Portrait to an Individual" on page 82.)

1. Access the chart you want to change. In the editing panel, choose an image type from the **Pictures** drop-down list:

    • Choose **Thumbnail** to use low-resolution thumbnail images.

    • Choose **Photo** to use the resolution of the actual assigned photo.

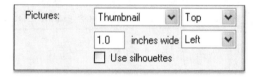

2. From the top drop-down list, choose how images are positioned next to fact boxes:

    • To align images with the middle of boxes, choose **Center**.

    • To align images with the top of boxes, choose **Top**.

    • To resize images to the same height as boxes, choose **Stretch**.

      Note: This option may cause your photos to look distorted.

    • To resize images to the same height as boxes (with cropped margins on the left and right side), choose **Zoom**.

3. From the bottom drop-down list, choose how images are displayed in fact boxes:

   - To display images on the left side, choose **Left.**

   - To display images on the right side, choose **Right.**

   - To display images as a background, choose **Behind.**

4. If you want to change the size of the photo or thumbnail, enter a size in the **Inches wide** field.

   Note: The larger the image is, the less space will be available for facts.

5. Click **Use silhouettes** if you want to display a silhouette icon for those individuals who don't have photographs.

Adding a Decorative Photo or Embellishments

You can personalize your charts and make them more appealing by adding family photographs, borders, and embellishments. You can add images from your computer, pictures in the Media Collection, or use the borders and images included in Family Tree Maker (fig. 9-13).

Figure 9-13

A family photo and embellishment on a descendant chart.

1. Access the chart you want to change. In the editing toolbar, click the **Insert image** button.

2. Choose an image using the drop-down list:

   • To use an image you've added to your tree, click **Insert from Media Collection**. The Find Media Item window opens. Choose an image and click **OK**.

   • To use an item on your computer's hard drive, click **Insert from File**. A file management window opens. Choose an image and click **Open**.

   Note: You'll find a variety of decorative images in the Embellishments folder located in the Family Tree Maker folder.

3. If you want to resize the image, click on the image. Move the cursor over the selection handles in the bottom-right corner. Then drag the image to the size you want.

4. If you want to change the position of the image, move the mouse over the image. When the cursor changes shape, click and drag the image to the location you want.

Changing the Header or Footer

You can define the headers and footers for each chart (the lines of text at the top and bottom of a chart).

1. Access the chart you want to change. In the editing toolbar, click the **Header/Footer** button.

The Header/Footer window opens.

2. Change the header and footer options as necessary:

   • **Chart note.** Enter a note you want to appear in the footer.

   • **Draw box around footer.** Click this checkbox to have the footer enclosed in a box.

   • **Print "Created with Family Tree Maker".** Click this checkbox to have this text added to the footer.

   • **Include submitter info.** If you have entered user information, click this checkbox to have it appear in the chart's footer. (To enter your user information, see page 254.)

- **Include date of printing.** Click this checkbox to include the current date in the footer.

- **Include time of printing.** Click this checkbox to include the current time in the footer.

- **Include page/chart numbers.** Click this checkbox to include page numbers in the chart. From the drop-down list, choose whether the number appears in the header or the footer.

  In **Starting number** enter the number of the chart's first page; in **Starting number for continuation charts**, enter the number of the second page of the chart.

3. Click **OK**.

Changing Formatting for a Chart

After you've decided what facts and individuals will be included in your chart, you can change the formatting to make eye-catching and creative charts. Family Tree Maker has the flexibility to let you change fonts, add colors and borders, change box sizes, and more.

Changing Layout Options

Depending on the number of individuals in your chart, facts you've included, etc., you may need to adjust the layout and spacing of a chart to best display each individual.

Note: Not every option is available in every chart.

1. Access the chart you want to change. The editing panel displays the options you can change.

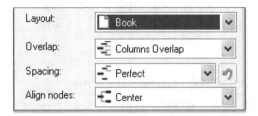

2. Change the chart's layout options as necessary:

- **Layout.** Choose **Book** to display the chart in pages suitable for using in a book; if a chart flows onto multiple pages, each page includes references to the generations continued on other pages. Choose **Poster** to display the chart in pages that can be linked together to form a poster (click the **Advanced** button to customize the poster format).

- **Overlap.** Change the horizontal spacing of a chart. Choose **No Overlap** to space columns equally; choose **Columns Overlap** to overlap columns slightly; choose **Only Root Overlaps** to overlap the primary individual's column with the parents' column; choose **Fishtail** to overlap all columns except for the last generation.

- **Spacing.** Change the vertical spacing of a chart. Choose **Perfect** to space rows evenly; choose **Collapsed** to space rows closer together; choose **Squished** to use minimal space between rows; choose **Custom** to use the settings in the Advanced poster format.

  Note: You might choose to collapse or squish the columns if you have many people in your tree and you're trying to fit them all on one page.

- **Align nodes.** Choose how lines connect individuals. Choose **Top** to use lines underneath names; choose **Center** to use lines centered next to each person's information; choose **Bezier** to use curved lines; choose **Straight** to use diagonal lines.

- **Center tree on page.** Click this checkbox to display the tree in the center of the page. If you are placing the chart in a bound book, you might not want to use this option. Instead, leave space for a left margin.

- **Display last descendant generation vertically.** Click this checkbox to list the last generation vertically under their parents.

- **Boxes overlap page breaks.** Click this checkbox if you want the chart spacing adjusted so that boxes that fall on a page break will not be split over two pages.

Adding Page Borders, Text Boxes, and Background Colors
You can personalize and enhance your charts by adding borders, background colors, and boxes.

1. Access the chart you want to change. In the editing toolbar, click the **Box and line styles** button.

2. To change the format of text boxes, click a group in the Boxes list, then change these options as necessary:

    *   Choose border, fill, and shadow colors from the drop-down lists.

    *   Click **Double line** if you want the box border to have two lines.

    *   Click **Rounded corners** if you want the boxes to have round corners.

    *   Click **All boxes same size** to make all boxes on the chart the same size.

    *   Click **Semi-transparent** to make the chart's background image or color partially visible through the boxes.

    *   Click **Use gradient fill** to make the box's fill color go from light to dark.

3. To change the size of boxes, enter the maximum width and height (in inches) for boxes in the "Book layout maximums."

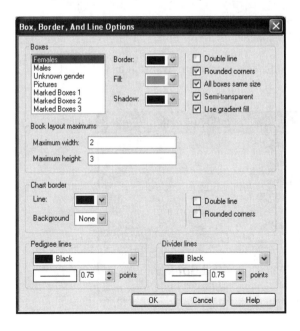

4. To change the format of lines that connect boxes together, choose the color of pedigree lines and divider lines from the drop-down lists. Then choose the thickness of the lines.

5. To add a border to the chart, choose a color from the **Line** drop-down list. Then click **Double line** if you want the border to contain two lines of color; click **Rounded corners** if you want the border lines to have round corners.

6. If you want to add a color background, choose the color from the **Background** drop-down list. (Choose "None" if you do not want a color background.)

7. Click **OK**.

Changing Fonts

You can change the appearance of the text in charts to make it more formal, more fun, or maybe just more readable.

1. Access the chart you want to change. In the editing toolbar, click the **Fonts** button.

2. In the **Items to format** list, click the text element, such as the chart title, you would like to change.

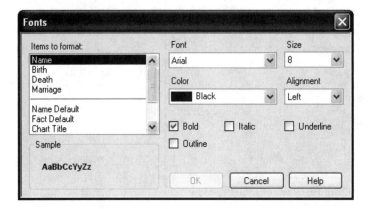

3. Choose a font from the **Font** drop-down list. You can also change the size of the text, its style, color, and alignment. The Sample box shows you how your font choices will appear in the chart.

4. Click **OK** to save your changes.

Using Chart Templates

Family Tree Maker comes with several templates you can use to dress up your family tree charts with artwork, creative color themes, formatted text boxes, and borders. And, you can also turn your own chart designs into templates.

Creating Your Own Template

After you have customized a chart with your favorite fonts and colors and changed the spacing and layout to make everyone fit perfectly on the page, you don't want to lose your settings. You can save your modifications as a template, and you won't have to recreate your changes if you want to use them on another chart.

1. After you have modified the chart, click the **Save settings** button in the editing toolbar.

2. Choose one of these options:

   • **Save as preferred template.** This option saves the current settings as the preferred template for all charts. However, this template isn't permanent; if you modify the preferred template, the old settings will be written over.

   • **Create new template.** This option lets you name the template and add it to the list of custom chart templates.

3. Click **OK**. To assign your template to a chart, see the next task.

Using a Custom Template

Maybe you want to create a beautiful pedigree chart to display on your wall, but you don't have an artistic bone in your body. Or maybe you just don't have any time. Family Tree Maker makes it easy to select an attractive template and instantly change the look of your chart.

You can apply custom templates to any chart. And if the results aren't exactly what you want, you can modify it.

1. Access the chart you want to apply a template to. Click the **Use saved settings** button in the editing toolbar.

2. Choose one of these template options:

    - **Default.** This is the original Family Tree Maker template.

    - **Preferred.** This is a template you have created and saved as your "preferred" template.

    - **Custom.** These are the custom templates found in Family Tree Maker (or templates you have created).

3. Click **OK**.

Saving Charts

You can save a specific chart that can be accessed in Family Tree Maker, or you can save a chart in different file formats you can export.

Saving a Specific Chart

After you've modified or customized a chart for an individual or family line you will probably want to save it. That way you can access the exact chart again without having to recreate it.

1. After you have modified the chart, click the **Save chart** button in the editing toolbar.

2. Enter a name for the chart in the **Chart name** field. Be sure to use a name that will distinguish the chart from others. For example, don't use generic terms like "Pedigree Chart" or "Relationship Chart."

3. Click **Save**.

TIP

To open a saved chart, go to the Collection tab on the Publish workspace. In Publication Types, click **Saved Charts**. Then double-click the chart you want to open.

Saving a Chart as a File

You may want to save a chart to a file format compatible with software other than Family Tree Maker; for example, as an image or PDF. These files can be easily shared with others or posted on a website.

1. Access the chart you want to save.

2. Click the **Share** button above the editing panel. From the drop-down list, choose one of these options:

   - **Export to PDF.** An Adobe PDF (Portable Document Format) is useful because PDFs keep the formatting you select. That way, if you print your chart or send it to a relative, the chart will look exactly as you see it on your monitor. You cannot make changes to the PDF within Family Tree Maker, and you need the Adobe Reader in order to view it. (Adobe Reader can be downloaded for free from the Adobe website.)

   - **Export to One Page PDF.** This option exports the chart as one page (regardless of size). You might want to use this if you are creating a poster-sized chart or having a chart printed at a copy store.

   - **Export to Image.** This option lets you create an image of the chart as a bitmap, JPEG, or other image format.

   Each format has its own export options you can choose from. After you choose a format type, you may be able to choose options such as page borders. Once you've made your selections, click **OK**. A file management window opens.

3. Navigate to the location you want. Then enter a name for the chart and click **Save**.

Printing a Chart

When you are done creating and customizing a chart, you may want to print it out. Family Tree Maker makes it easy to choose setup options and print a chart.

1. Access the chart you want to print.

2. Click the **Print** button above the editing panel. Just like printing from any other application, you can choose a printer, select the number of copies, and choose a page range.

3. Click **Print**.

Sharing a Chart

Family Tree Maker lets you share charts with others—via e-mail—as a PDF.

> Note: You must be connected to the Internet and have a desktop e-mail program to use this feature.

1. Access the chart you want to e-mail.

2. Click the **Share** button above the editing panel. From the drop-down list, choose **Send as PDF.**

3. Use the preview window to make sure the chart looks the way you want. Then click **Send as PDF.**

4. Change any options as necessary and click **OK.**

5. Navigate to the location where you want to save the chart. Then enter a name for the chart and click **Save.** Family Tree Maker opens a new e-mail (with the file attached) in your default e-mail program.

6. Send the e-mail as you would any other.

Chapter Ten
Running Reports

Reports are mainstays of family historians. And Family Tree Maker includes a number of reports to help you organize and understand all the information you have entered in your tree. You can create detailed reports about a single family unit, such as the family group sheet; relationship reports that show marriage events or parentage facts; bibliographies and source usage reports that help you keep track of your research; and more.

Each report can be customized—options differ by report. You can change fonts, add background images, and add headers and footers. Simply select the type of report and format you want—Family Tree Maker does the work for you.

Genealogy Reports

Genealogy reports are a staple for serious family historians. These narrative reports contain facts and biographical details about individuals and families in your tree. Relationships between individuals are shown using numbering systems that are unique to each type of report. You can choose from ancestor-ordered reports (Ahnentafels) or descendant-ordered reports.

Ahnentafel

The Ahnentafel (a German word meaning "ancestor table") is basically a numbered list of individuals (fig. 10-1). Its format is ancestor-ordered, meaning that it starts with one individual and moves backward in time to that individual's ancestors. This type of report isn't used frequently because it records two family lines at the same time.

Figure 10-1

An Ahnentafel
(ancestor
report).

Ancestors of Emma Gedge

Generation 1

1. **Emma Gedge**, daughter of William Gedge and Rachel Bush was born on 30 Aug 1863 in Utah, USA. She died on 11 Dec 1906 in St George, Washington, Utah, USA. She married **Samuel G. Spencer** on 21 Dec 1883.

Generation 2

2. **William Gedge**, son of George Gedge and Lucy Kybird was born on 01 Jan 1830 in Old Buckenham, Norfolk, England. He died on 30 Dec 1912 in Taylorsville, Salt Lake, Utah, USA. He married **Rachel Bush** on 22 Nov 1855 in Guiltcross, Norfolk, England.

3. **Rachel Bush**, daughter of Robb Bush and Mary Rush was born on 10 Oct 1833 in Deopham, Norfolk, England. She died on 15 Mar 1911 in Salt Lake City, Salt Lake, Utah, USA.

Rachel Bush and William Gedge had the following children:

    i.   Leah Gedge was born about 1859 in Old Buckenham, Norfolk, England. She died on 13 Aug 1862 in Wyoming or Nebraska.

    ii.   Mary Gedge was born on 01 Aug 1862 in Nebraska, USA. She died on 30 Aug 1862 in Wyoming, USA. She married.

    iii.   Lois Gedge was born on 01 Aug 1862 in Nebraska, USA. She died on 30 Aug 1862 in Wyoming, USA. She married.

+1.   iv.   Emma Gedge was born on 30 Aug 1863 in Utah, USA. She died on 11 Dec 1906 in St George, Washington, Utah, USA. She married Samuel G. Spencer on 21 Dec

Descendant Report

A descendant report (fig. 10-2) is a narrative genealogy report that includes basic facts and biographical information about an individual. It is descendant-ordered, meaning that it starts with one individual and moves forward in time through that individual's descendants. Family Tree Maker gives you four different report options: Register, NGSQ, Henry, and d'Aboville. The main difference between these report types is the numbering system that is used.

Figure 10-2

A Register
descendant
report.

Descendants of James Hoyt

Generation 1

1. JAMES¹ HOYT was born on 19 Sep 1807 in Stamford, Fairfield, Connecticut, USA. He died in 1902. He married (1) MARIA HITCHCOCK on 19 Sep 1833. She was born in 1815 in New York City, New York, USA. She died on 13 Mar 1850 in Illinois, USA. He married (2) ELIZA JANE MATHIS on 28 Jul 1853. She was born in 1830. She died in 1924.

James Hoyt and Maria Hitchcock had the following children:

+2.   i.   JULIA² HOYT was born on 06 Sep 1834 in Chillicothe, Ross, Ohio, USA. She died on 28 Jul 1923. She married JOHN W. BOBBITT on 18 Oct 1852, son of Isham Drury Bobbitt and Cyntha Ann Haggard. He was born on 09 Jun 1832 in Kentucky, USA. He died on 24 Aug 1909 in Dawson, Richardson, Nebraska, USA.

    ii.   ELEANOR HOYT was born on 30 Mar 1837 in Chillicothe, Ross, Ohio, USA. She died on 25 Jul 1838. She married.

    iii.   JAMES HENRY HOYT was born on 01 May 1839 in Lacon, Marshall, Illinois, USA. He died on 01 Oct 1922 in Golden City, Barton, Missouri, USA. He married ESTHER READY.

        Notes for James Henry Hoyt:
        Living in Martinsburg, Missouri, in 1871

    iv.   SARAH ELIZABETH HOYT was born on 06 Jul 1841 in Marshall County, Illinois, USA. She died on 13 Feb 1929. She married SAMUEL CLIFFORD.

    v.   ANN MARIA HOYT was born on 20 Jul 1843 in Marshall County, Illinois, USA. She

Person Reports

Person reports focus on an individual in your tree. You can create a report of all the facts and sources you have recorded for a person, create a report of research notes or tasks in your Research To-Do list, or create a custom report.

Custom Report

Custom reports (fig. 10-3) let you create reports with your own criteria. For example, you can create a custom report of birthplaces or causes of death if you have recorded that information for several individuals in your tree. A custom report defaults to a list of all individuals, birth dates, and death dates, so you can begin to customize it with all information intact.

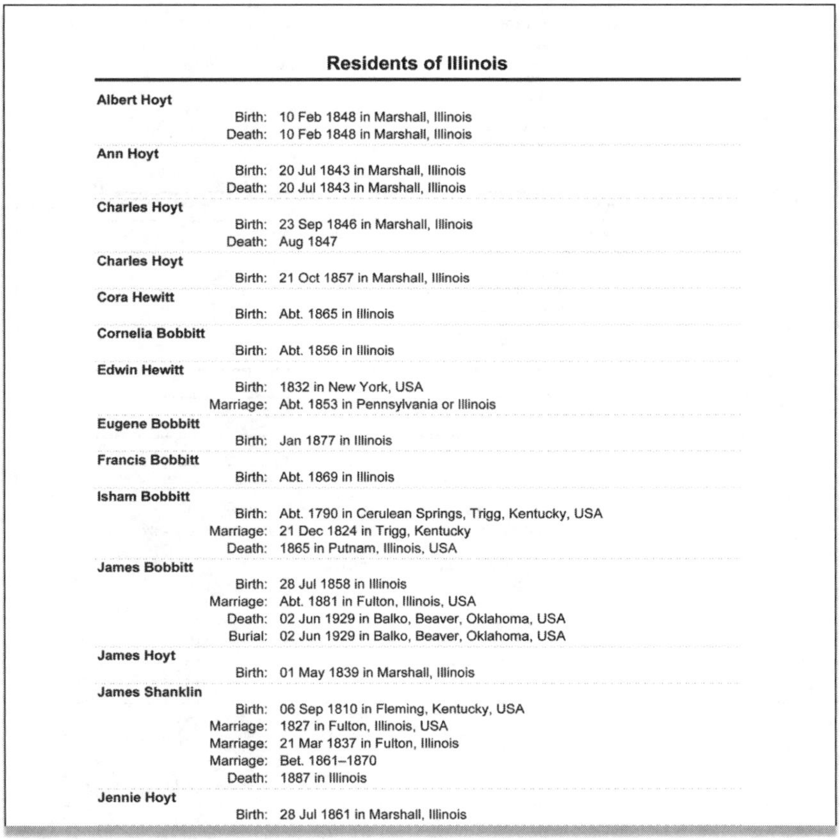

Residents of Illinois

Albert Hoyt
Birth: 10 Feb 1848 in Marshall, Illinois
Death: 10 Feb 1848 in Marshall, Illinois

Ann Hoyt
Birth: 20 Jul 1843 in Marshall, Illinois
Death: 20 Jul 1843 in Marshall, Illinois

Charles Hoyt
Birth: 23 Sep 1846 in Marshall, Illinois
Death: Aug 1847

Charles Hoyt
Birth: 21 Oct 1857 in Marshall, Illinois

Cora Hewitt
Birth: Abt. 1865 in Illinois

Cornelia Bobbitt
Birth: Abt. 1856 in Illinois

Edwin Hewitt
Birth: 1832 in New York, USA
Marriage: Abt. 1853 in Pennsylvania or Illinois

Eugene Bobbitt
Birth: Jan 1877 in Illinois

Francis Bobbitt
Birth: Abt. 1869 in Illinois

Isham Bobbitt
Birth: Abt. 1790 in Cerulean Springs, Trigg, Kentucky, USA
Marriage: 21 Dec 1824 in Trigg, Kentucky
Death: 1865 in Putnam, Illinois, USA

James Bobbitt
Birth: 28 Jul 1858 in Illinois
Marriage: Abt. 1881 in Fulton, Illinois, USA
Death: 02 Jun 1929 in Balko, Beaver, Oklahoma, USA
Burial: 02 Jun 1929 in Balko, Beaver, Oklahoma, USA

James Hoyt
Birth: 01 May 1839 in Marshall, Illinois

James Shanklin
Birth: 06 Sep 1810 in Fleming, Kentucky, USA
Marriage: 1827 in Fulton, Illinois, USA
Marriage: 21 Mar 1837 in Fulton, Illinois
Marriage: Bet. 1861–1870
Death: 1887 in Illinois

Jennie Hoyt
Birth: 28 Jul 1861 in Marshall, Illinois

Figure 10-3

A custom report showing all individuals who lived in Illinois.

Individual Report

The Individual Report (fig. 10-4) lists every fact and source you have recorded for a specific individual.

Figure 10-4

An Individual Report.

Individual Report for Cyrus Henry Gold

Individual Summary:	Cyrus Gold
Sex:	Male
Father:	Joseph Gold
Mother:	Sarah Thompson

Individual Facts:

Name:	Cyrus Gold
Birth:	01 May 1848 in Birmingham, Warwick, England [1]
Death:	27 Mar 1930 in Salt Lake City, Salt Lake, Utah, USA [2]

Shared Facts: Mary Willis

Marriage:	27 Mar 1871 in Salt Lake City, Salt Lake, Utah, USA [3]
Children:	Sarah Gold
	Cyrus Gold
	Thomas Gold
	Abraham Gold
	Alma Gold
	Lehi Gold
	Helaman Gold
	Elmina Gold
	Mary Gold
	Henry Gold

Shared Facts: Louisa Newman

Marriage:	08 Aug 1904 in Salt Lake City, Salt Lake, Utah, USA [4]
Children:	Earnest Gold
	Louisa Gold
	Ruth Gold
	Gertrude Gold
	Annie Gold
	Edwin Gold
	John Gold

Notes:

Person Notes:	[no notes]

Sources:

1 England, Register of Births, Cyrus Henry Gold.; General Register Office, Somerset House London.
2 Utah, State Board of Health, Death Certificates, Cyrus Henry Gold. File no. 599.
3 Desert Gedge Johnson, "Mary Willis- Wife of Cyrus Henry Gold"; Personal writings (; privately held by Tana L. Pedersen (copy)).
4 Salt Lake, Utah, Gold and Newman. Vol. P. Page 57. Marriage ID 354782.

Research Note Report

The Research Note Report (fig. 10-5) displays research notes you've entered for individuals in your tree.

Research Note Report

Elizabeth Gentry
Birth - Death: 14 Aug 1731 - 28 Jul 1820
Research Note: Had ten children, six of whom were sons.

Bartlett Haggard
Birth - Death: 04 Feb 1764 - 18 May 1846
Research Note: Bartlett and David were twins and married sisters.

Martha Haggard
Birth - Death: 1795 - 1871
Research Note: Married names of Routt and Newton.

Edwin Hewitt
Birth - Death: 1833 - ?
Research Note: Edwin is living with the Main family in Pennsylvania in 1850. Was he living with them at the time of the 1840 census? When did he move to Pennsylvania and why?

Maria Hitchcock
Birth - Death: 1815 - 13 Mar 1850
Research Note: County histories show that Maria married James in New York City abt. 1837. Need to see if New York City kept marriage records that early. Census

Figure 10-5

A report showing all research notes entered in a tree.

LDS Ordinances Report

The LDS Ordinances Report (fig. 10-6) is useful for members of The Church of Jesus Christ of Latter-day Saints (LDS church) and displays LDS-specific ordinances such as baptisms and sealings.

LDS Ordinances

Gedge, Herbert Bush
Birth: 10 Nov 1872 in Brighton, Salt Lake, Utah
Marriage: 20 Nov 1895 in Salt Lake City, Salt Lake, Utah
Death: 08 Sep 1942 in Salt Lake, Salt Lake City, Utah
Baptism (LDS): 10 Nov 1880
Endowment (LDS): 20 Nov 1895

Gedge, Phoebe Gold
Birth: 27 May 1900 in Salt Lake City, Salt Lake, Utah
Marriage: 15 Sep 1926 in Salt Lake City, Utah
Death: 28 Dec 1948 in Salt Lake City, Salt Lake, Utah
Endowment (LDS): 15 Sep 1926 in Salt Lake City, UT, USA

Gold, Sarah Hannah
Birth: 03 Dec 1873 in Salt Lake City, Utah
Marriage: 20 Nov 1895 in Salt Lake City, Salt Lake, Utah
Death: 05 Nov 1963 in Salt Lake City, Utah
Baptism (LDS): 03 Jan 1882

Figure 10-6

An LDS Ordinances Report.

Task List

A task list (fig. 10-7) displays all research tasks you've entered into your To-Do list. You can see each task's priority level, categories you've assigned it to, and creation and due dates. You can also choose to filter the report by tasks that have already been completed.

Figure 10-7

A list of research tasks entered in a tree.

Task List

☐	Write to Berks County Historical Society for Reed/Rieth church records	Priority: High Owner: General Task Categories: Reed Date Created: 3/24/2010 Date Due: 3/26/2010
☐	Write to Peoria County for Milton Hewitt's death record.	Priority: High Owner: General Task Categories: Hewitt Date Created: 2/17/2010 Date Due: 4/30/2010
☐	Look for marriage record for Joseph Thompson and "Jane" between 1840 and 1845 in Warwickshire, England	Priority: Medium Owner: General Task Categories: Records Date Created: 3/24/2010 Date Due: 6/30/2010
☐	Look up name of Brighton church book (GEDGE family) in Family History Library for source citation.	Priority: Medium Owner: General Task Categories: Gedge Date Created: 2/17/2010 Date Due: 4/30/2010
☐	Send Aunt Chris an email about the family photos.	Priority: Low Owner: General Task Categories: Communication Date Created: 2/17/2010 Date Due: 6/30/2010
☒	Find out when Phoebe Gedge went to the U of U and see if you can get a diploma.	Priority: Medium Owner: General Task Categories: Gedge Date Created: 2/17/2010 Date Due: 8/31/2010

Data Errors Report

Family Tree Maker can search your tree and create a report of all the problems it discovers. The Data Errors Report (fig. 10-8) lists all instances where there is missing data or where Family Tree Maker believes there may be a mistake. This includes nonsensical dates (e.g., an individual being born before his or her parents were born), empty fields, duplicate individuals, typos, and more. (For more information, see "Running the Data Errors Report" on page 264.)

Data Errors Report

Name	Birth Date	Potential Error
Anna Gedge	05 Sep 1865	The burial date occurred before his/her death.
Nathan Gedge	Abt. 1971	The birth date occurred after his/her mother was 60. The birth date occurred after his/her mother died. The birth date occurred after his/her father was 80. The birth date occurred more than one year after his/her father died.
Mette Katrina Pedersen		The individual has the same last name as her husband, Niels Pedersen.
Oliver Cowdrey Pedersen	Abt. 1891	Arrival date occurred before individual's birth date.

Figure 10-8

A Data Errors Report.

Surname Report

The Surname Report (fig. 10-9) lists the surnames in your tree, including the total number of individuals with that surname, the number of males and females with that surname, and the earliest and most recent year a surname appears in your tree.

Surname Report

Surname	Count	Male	Female	Earliest	Most recent
Hoyt	34	18	16	1740	1861
Gold	31	16	15	1825	1908
Bobbitt	27	12	15	1793	1909
Haggard	25	14	11	1678	1813
Gedge	23	11	12	1830	1914
Reed	15	7	8	1774	1901
Pedersen	12	7	4	1821	1973
Peterson	10	6	4	1888	1905
Shanklin	7	3	4	1810	1866
Thompson	7	4	3	1796	1835
Bennington	5	1	3	1802	1812
Hewitt	4	2	2	1833	1865
Rieth	4	2	2	1822	1861
Dawson	3	1	2	1764	1764
Gentry	3	1	2	1731	1731

Figure 10-9

A Surname Report sorted by name count.

Timeline

A timeline (fig. 10-10) lists all the events you've entered for an individual. Each event shows the date and location of the event and the person's age at the time. You can also choose to include important events in an individual's immediate family (such as birth, marriage, and death) and historical events.

Figure 10-10

A timeline for an individual.

Timeline Report for John W. Bobbitt

	Yr/Age	Event	Date/Place
	1832	Birth	09 Jun 1832
			Kentucky, USA
	1834	Birth (Spouse)	06 Sep 1834
	2	Julia Hoyt	Chillicothe, Ross, Ohio, USA
	1850	1850 U.S. Census	1850
	17		Tazewell County, Illinois, USA
	1852	Marriage	18 Oct 1852
	20	Julia Hoyt	
	1854	Birth (Son)	Abt. 1854
	21	Seymour Bobbitt	Illinois, USA
	1857	Birth (Daughter)	Mar 1857
	24	Cornelia O. Bobbitt	Illinois, USA
	1858	Birth (Son)	28 Jul 1858
	26	James Clarence Bobbitt	Illinois, USA
	1860	1860 U.S. Census	1860
	27		Roberts, Marshall, Illinois, USA
	1861	Birth (Son)	Abt. 1861
	28	Willis R. Bobbitt	Illinois, USA
	1862	Death (Father)	14 Nov 1862
	30	Isham Drury Bobbitt	
	1863	Birth (Daughter)	Abt. 1863
	30	Sarah Eleanor Bobbitt	Illinois, USA
	1868	Birth (Son)	1868
	35	Francis Marion Bobbitt	Illinois, USA
	1870	1870 U.S. Census	1870
	37		Roberts, Marshall, Illinois, USA
	1872	Birth (Daughter)	02 Mar 1872
	39	Unknown Female Bobbitt	Varna, Marshall, Illinois, USA
	1872	Birth (Daughter)	03 Mar 1872
	39	Jessie Julia Bobbitt	Illinois, USA
	1873	Marriage (Daughter)	02 Feb 1873
	40	Cornelia O. Bobbitt	Varna, Marshall, Illinois, USA

Relationship Reports

Relationship reports are just what they sound like; they show the relationships between different individuals and families in your tree.

Family Group Sheet

A family group sheet (fig. 10-11) is one of the most commonly used reports in genealogy. It is a detailed report about a single family (primarily the parents and children of a family, although it also includes the names of the main couple's parents), including names, birth information, death information, marriage information, notes, and sources. If the individual has more than one spouse, a second family group sheet will show that family unit.

Family Group Sheet for Margaret Rebecca Shanklin

Husband:		James Clarence Bobbitt
	Birth:	28 Jul 1858 in Illinois, USA
	Death:	02 Jun 1929
	Burial:	Balko, Beaver, Oklahoma, USA
	Marriage:	20 Feb 1882 in Marshall County, Illinois, USA
	Father:	John W. Bobbitt
	Mother:	Julia Hoyt

Wife:		Margaret Rebecca Shanklin
	Birth:	12 Jul 1863 in Illinois, USA
	Death:	29 Mar 1944
	Burial:	Balko, Beaver, Oklahoma, USA
	Father:	William Bennington Shanklin
	Mother:	Charity Perry

Children:

1 F	Name:	Charity Bobbitt
	Birth:	10 Mar 1883 in Nebraska, USA
	Death:	May 1982
	Spouse:	William Burdette Crossman

2 M	Name:	James Leslie Bobbitt
	Birth:	19 Sep 1884 in Nebraska, USA
	Death:	22 Mar 1971
	Burial:	Balko, Beaver, Oklahoma, USA

3 F	Name:	Mary E "Mollie" Bobbitt
	Birth:	Apr 1886 in Nebraska, USA
	Death:	1966
	Spouse:	Parsons

4 F	Name:	Bessie Anita Bobbitt
	Birth:	14 Dec 1888 in Nebraska, USA
	Death:	18 Jan 1978
	Burial:	Centerton, Benton, Arkansas, USA
	Marriage:	21 Feb 1910 in Carrier, Garfield, Oklahoma, USA
	Spouse:	Fred D. Shepard

5 F	Name:	Alta Maud Bobbitt
	Birth:	09 Feb 1892 in Kansas, USA
	Death:	04 Nov 1987 in Cherokee, Alfalfa, Oklahoma, USA
	Spouse:	Alonzo W. Ford

6 M	Name:	Arthur Leroy Bobbitt
	Birth:	24 Aug 1897
	Death:	05 Jun 1993
	Burial:	Oklahoma City, Oklahoma, Oklahoma, USA
	Spouse:	Myrtle Goodman

Figure 10-11

A family group sheet.

Kinship Report

The Kinship Report (fig. 10-12) helps you determine how individuals in your database are related to a specific person.

Kinship Report for Maria Hitchcock

Name:	Birth Date:	Relationship:	Civil:	Canon:
(Hoyt), John Hait	24 Nov 1740	Father of father-in-law		
Bobbitt, Alta M.	09 Feb 1892	Great granddaughter	III	3
Bobbitt, Arthur L.	24 Aug 1897	Great grandson	III	3
Bobbitt, Bessie A.	14 Dec 1888	Great granddaughter	III	3
Bobbitt, Charity M.	10 Mar 1883	Great granddaughter	III	3
Bobbitt, Cornelia	Abt. 1856	Granddaughter	II	2
Bobbitt, Eugene A.	Jan 1877	Grandson	II	2
Bobbitt, Fern Edna	25 Feb 1909	Great granddaughter	III	3
Bobbitt, Francis M.	Abt. 1869	Grandson	II	2
Bobbitt, James Clarence	28 Jul 1858	Grandson	II	2
Bobbitt, James Leslie	19 Sep 1884	Great grandson	III	3
Bobbitt, Jessie	Abt. 1873	Grandson	II	2
Bobbitt, John W.	09 Jun 1832	Son-in-law		
Bobbitt, Lorine	04 Jun 1906	Great granddaughter	III	3
Bobbitt, Mary Eliza	10 Apr 1886	Great granddaughter	III	3
Bobbitt, Maurine	04 Jun 1906	Great granddaughter	III	3

Marriage Report

The Marriage Report (fig. 10-13) shows information about each marriage in your tree. Unlike other reports, you cannot choose which individuals are included; Family Tree Maker automatically includes the names of husbands and wives, their marriage dates, and their relationship status.

Marriage Report

Husband:	Wife:	Marriage Date:	Relation:
Andersen, Peder Christian	Nielsdatter, Maren		Spouse - Ongoing
Andersen, Peder Christian	Peterson, M. K.		Spouse - Ongoing
Bennington, William Jr.	Smith, Margaret	16 Apr 1793	Spouse - Ongoing
Bobbitt, Isham Drury	Haggard, Cyntha Ann	21 Dec 1824	Spouse - Ongoing
Bobbitt, James Clarence	Shanklin, Margaret Rebecca	20 Feb 1882	Spouse - Ongoing
Bobbitt, John W.	Hoyt, Julia	18 Oct 1852	Spouse - Ongoing
Bush, Robb	Rush, Mary		Spouse - Ongoing
Dawson, Martin	Carter, Elizabeth		Spouse - Ongoing
Gedge, George	Kybird, Lucy		Spouse - Ongoing
Gedge, Herbert Bush	Gold, Sarah Hannah	20 Nov 1895	Spouse - Ongoing
Gedge, Reames	Kybird, Lucy		Spouse - Ongoing
Gedge, William	Bush, Rachel	22 Nov 1855	Spouse - Ongoing
Gold, Cyrus Henry	Newman, Louisa Fanny	08 Aug 1904	Spouse - Ongoing
Gold, Cyrus Henry	Willis, Mary	27 Mar 1871	Spouse - Ongoing
Gold, Joseph	Thompson, Sarah	27 Jan 1845	Spouse - Ongoing

Outline Descendant Report

The Outline Descendant Report (fig. 10-14) starts with an ancestor and outlines each generation of descendants; you can even select the number of generations to show in the report.

Outline Descendant Report for Abigail Hait

..... 1 Abigail Hait b: 09 Oct 1740 in Stamford, Fairfield, Connecticut, USA, d: 27 Feb 1796 in Stamford, Fairfield, Connecticut, USA
..... + John Hoyt b: 24 Nov 1740 in Stamford, Fairfield, Connecticut, USA, m: 31 Dec 1761, d: 01 Mar 1825
.... 2 Samuel Hoyt b: 08 Nov 1762 in Stamford, Fairfield, Connecticut, USA, d: 22 Sep 1838 in Stamford, Fairfield, Connecticut, USA
.... 2 William Hoyt b: 01 Aug 1764 in Stamford, Fairfield, Connecticut, USA, d: 25 Aug 1828
.... 2 John Hoyt b: 02 Dec 1765 in Stamford, Fairfield, Connecticut, USA, d: 15 Dec 1812 in Burlington, Chittenden, Vermont, USA
.... 2 Abigail Hoyt b: 31 Oct 1767 in Stamford, Fairfield, Connecticut, USA, d: 26 Aug 1840 in Norwalk, Fairfield, Connecticut, USA
.... 2 Benjamin Hoyt b: 19 Feb 1769 in Stamford, Fairfield, Connecticut, USA, d: 21 Nov 1813
.... + Elizabeth Reed b: 15 Nov 1774, m: 23 Dec 1792, d: 11 Jun 1818
.... 3 Sarah Hoyt b: 23 Feb 1794 in Tarrytown, Westchester, New York, USA
.... 3 Seymour Hoyt b: 22 Mar 1796 in Stamford, Fairfield, Connecticut, USA, d: 29 Oct 1866 in Stamford, Fairfield, Connecticut, USA
.... 3 Benjamin Hoyt b: 28 Jul 1798 in Stamford, Fairfield, Connecticut, USA, d: 13 Feb 1801 in Stamford, Fairfield, Connecticut, USA
.... 3 Elizabeth Hoyt b: 05 Aug 1800 in Stamford, Fairfield, Connecticut, USA, d: Aft. 1871
.... 3 Benjamin Hoyt b: 26 Nov 1802 in Stamford, Fairfield, Connecticut, USA
.... 3 Emeline Hoyt b: 02 Jun 1805 in Stamford, Fairfield, Connecticut, USA, d: 09 Jan 1854

Figure 10-14

An Outline Descendant Report.

Parentage Report

The Parentage Report (fig. 10-15) lists each individual, the individual's parents, and the relationship between the individual and parents (e.g., natural, adopted, foster).

Parentage Report

Name	Parents	Relationship
Andersen, Peder Christian		
Bell, Abigail		
Bell, Permelia		
Bennington, Sarah	Bennington, William Jr.	Natural
	Smith, Margaret	Natural
Bennington, William Jr.		
Bobbitt, Isham Drury		
Bobbitt, James Clarence	Bobbitt, John W.	Natural
	Hoyt, Julia	Natural
Bobbitt, John W.	Bobbitt, Isham Drury	Natural
	Haggard, Cyntha Ann	Natural
Bobbitt, Maurine	Bobbitt, James Clarence	Natural
	Shanklin, Margaret Rebecca	Natural
Bush, Rachel	Bush, Robb	Natural
	Rush, Mary	Natural
Bush, Robb		

Figure 10-15

A Parentage Report.

Place Usage Report

The Place Usage Report (fig. 10-16) lists the locations you have entered into your tree and each person associated with that location. You can also choose to include the specific events, such as birth or marriage, that occurred in that location.

Figure 10-16

A Place Usage Report.

Place Usage Report

Albemarle County, Virginia, USA
Haggard, David
Birth: 1763
Haggard, Nathaniel
Birth: 21 Nov 1723

Ålborg, Nordjylland, Denmark
Pedersen, Mette
Res: May 1924
Pedersen, Mette Katrina
Emigr: 05 Oct 1899
Pedersen, Niels
Emigr: 20 Apr 1899
Pedersen, Oliver Cowdery
Birth: 26 Apr 1891
Emigr: 05 Oct 1899

Aston Manor, Warwick, England
Gold, Joseph
Occu: 1861 Bricklayer

Aston, Warwick, England
Gold, Joseph
Marr: 27 Jan 1845
Marr: 30 Jun 1861
Marr: 20 Jun 1861
Thompson, Sarah
Marr: 27 Jan 1845

Balko, Beaver, Oklahoma, USA
Bobbitt, James Clarence
Burial: Pleasant Hill Cemetery
Hewitt, Jessie Izetta
Burial: Pleasant Hill Cemetery
Shanklin, Margaret Rebecca
Burial: Pleasant Hill Cemetery

Beaver County, Oklahoma, USA
Bobbitt, Maurine
Marr: 18 Aug 1923
Reed, Harold Arthur
Marr: 18 Aug 1923

Bell Plain, Marshall, Illinois, USA
Bennington, Sarah
1860:   1860
Bobbitt, John W.
Pol: 1877 Assessor
Shanklin, James A.
1860:   1860
1870:   1870
Shanklin, Margaret Rebecca
1870:   1870

Media Reports

The media reports in Family Tree Maker let you view media items individually or compiled into groups.

Media Item Report

You can create a Media Item Report (fig. 10-17) about any media item you have included in your tree, including its caption, date of origin, description, and any individuals associated with the item. This report is most useful for image files.

Maurine and Lorine Bobbitt

Caption: Maurine and Lorine Bobbitt
Date: 1905
Categories: Group Portrait

Description: A photo of twins Maurine (left) and Lorine (right) Bobbitt that was taken three months after their birth in the summer of 1905.

Links:

Person: Bobbitt, Maurine
Person: Bobbitt, Lorine

Figure 10-17

A Media Item Report.

Media Usage Report

The Media Usage Report (fig. 10-18) shows a thumbnail of every media item in your tree and lists its name and location and shows which sources, facts, and individuals the item is linked to.

Figure 10-18

A Media Usage Report.

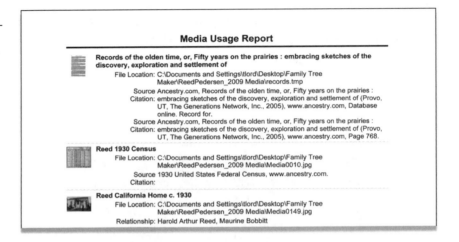

Photo Album

The photo album (fig. 10-19) shows a basic summary of an individual's life events, such as birth and death dates, and also includes all photos associated with the person.

Figure 10-19

A photo album for an individual.

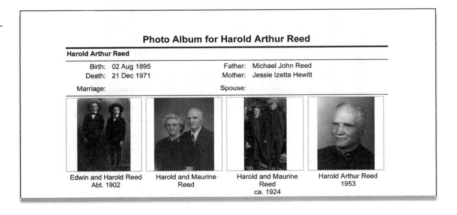

Source Reports

Because making your family history accurate and complete is important, Family Tree Maker includes several reports that help you view how you've sourced facts in your tree.

Bibliography

The bibliography (fig. 10-20) gives a detailed list of all the sources you used in your research. This helps others locate and examine the resources you used.

Figure 10-20

An annotated source bibliography.

Source Bibliography

E. Duis, The good old times in McLean County, Illinois: containing two hundred and sixty-one sketches of old settlers, a complete history (The Leader Publishing and Printing House, 1874).

Mrs. Jennie (Haggard) Ray, History of the Haggard family in England and America 1433 to 1899 to 1938 (, 1938), Found on Google Books.

1930 U.S. census, population schedule. California. Santa Clara. NARA microfilm publication , roll 219. Washington, D.C.: National Archives and Records Administration, n.d.

A Genealogical History of the Hoyt, Haight, and Hight Families (Chicago, Illinois, The S.J. Clarke Publishing Company, 1886), Family History Library, 35 North West Temple Street Salt Lake City, Utah 84150-3440.

Altalaha Lutheran Cemetery (Rehrersburg, Berks, Pennsylvania). Grave markers. [Source includes media item(s)]

Ancestry.com and The Church of Jesus Christ of Latter-day Saints, 1880 United States Federal Census (Provo, UT, USA, Ancestry.com Operations Inc, 2005), www.ancestry.com, United States of America, Bureau of the Census, Tenth Census of the United States, 1880, Washington, D.C.: National Archives and Records Administration, 1880.

Ancestry.com, 1810 United States Federal Census (Provo, UT, USA, Ancestry.com Operations Inc, 2010), www.ancestry.com.

Ancestry.com, 1841 England Census (Provo, UT, USA, Ancestry.com Operations Inc, 2006), www.ancestry.com, Census Returns of England and Wales, 1841, Kew, Surrey, England: The National Archives of the UK (TNA): Public Record Office (PRO), 1841.

Ancestry.com, 1850 United States Federal Census (Provo, UT, USA, The Generations Network, Inc., 2005), www.ancestry.com, United States of America, Bureau of the Census, Seventh Census of the United States, 1850, Washington, D.C.: National Archives and Records Administration, 1850.

Ancestry.com, 1851 England Census (Ancestry.com).

Ancestry.com, 1851 England Census (Provo, UT, USA, Ancestry.com Operations Inc, 2005), www.ancestry.com, Census Returns of England and Wales, 1851, Kew, Surrey, England: The National Archives of the UK (TNA): Public Record Office (PRO), 1851.

Ancestry.com, 1860 United States Federal Census (Provo, UT, USA, The Generations Network, Inc., 2004), www.ancestry.com, United States of America, Bureau of the Census, Eighth Census of the United States, 1860, Washington, D.C.: National Archives and Records Administration, 1860.

Ancestry.com, 1861 England Census (Ancestry.com).

Ancestry.com, 1861 England Census (Provo, UT, USA, Ancestry.com Operations Inc, 2005), www.ancestry.com, Census Returns of England and Wales, 1861, Kew, Surrey, England: The National Archives of the UK (TNA): Public Record Office (PRO), 1861.

Ancestry.com, 1870 United States Federal Census (Provo, UT, USA, The Generations Network, Inc., 2003), www.ancestry.com.

Ancestry.com, 1880 United States Federal Census.

Ancestry.com, 1900 United States Federal Census (Provo, UT, USA, The Generations Network, Inc., 2004), www.ancestry.com.

Ancestry.com, 1910 United States Federal Census (Provo, UT, USA, The Generations Network, Inc., 2006), www.ancestry.com.

Documented Facts Report

The Documented Facts Report (fig. 10-21) lists all of the events for which you have entered source information. Conversely, you can choose to show all of the events for which you do not have source information and use the report as a reminder of what you still need to research.

Documented Facts

Bennington, Sarah
1860:	1860 in Bell Plain, Marshall, Illinois, USA	
	1	Ancestry.com, 1860 United States Federal Census (Provo, UT, USA, The Generations Network, Inc., 2004), www.ancestry.com, Database online. Year: 1860; Census Place: Bell Plain, Marshall, Illinois; Roll: ; Page: ; Image:. Record for Sarah Shanklin. [Source citation includes media item(s)]
Birth:	17 Feb 1812	
	1	Ancestry.com, 1860 United States Federal Census (Provo, UT, USA, The Generations Network, Inc., 2004), www.ancestry.com, Database online. Year: 1860; Census Place: Bell Plain, Marshall, Illinois; Roll: ; Page: ; Image:. Record for Sarah Shanklin. [Source citation includes media item(s)]
	2	Pattonsburg-Moss Cemetery (Pattonsburg, Marshall, Illinois), James A. Shanklin and Sarah. [Source citation includes media item(s)]
Burial:	Pattonsburg, Marshall, Illinois, USA; Pattonsburg-Moss Cemetery	
	1	Pattonsburg-Moss Cemetery (Pattonsburg, Marshall, Illinois), James A. Shanklin and Sarah. [Source citation includes media item(s)]
Death:	13 Aug 1863	
	1	Pattonsburg-Moss Cemetery (Pattonsburg, Marshall, Illinois), James A. Shanklin and Sarah. [Source citation includes media item(s)]

Source Usage Report

The Source Usage Report (fig. 10-22) includes each source you have created and lists the individuals and facts associated with that source. This report

Source Usage Report

Source Title: **1850 United States Federal Census**
Repository: www.ancestry.com
Citation: Ancestry.com, 1850 United States Federal Census (Provo, UT, USA, The Generations Network, Inc., 2005), www.ancestry.com, Database online. Year: 1850; Census Place: District 1, Fleming, Kentucky; Roll: M432_199; Page: 346A; Image:. Record for Sarah Shanklin. [Source citation includes media item(s)]
Bennington, Sarah

Source Title: **1860 United States Federal Census**
Repository: www.ancestry.com
Citation: Ancestry.com, 1860 United States Federal Census (Provo, UT, USA, The Generations Network, Inc., 2004), www.ancestry.com, Database online. Year: 1860; Census Place: Bell Plain, Marshall, Illinois; Roll: ; Page: ; Image:. Record for Sarah Shanklin. [Source citation includes media item(s)]
Bennington, Sarah

Source Title: **A Genealogical History of the Hoyt, Haight, and Hight Families**
Repository: Family History Library
Citation: A Genealogical History of the Hoyt, Haight, and Hight Families (Chicago, Illinois, The S.J. Clarke Publishing Company, 1886), Family History Library, 35 North West Temple Street
Salt Lake City, Utah 84150-3440, pg 477. [Source citation includes media item(s)]
Hoyt, James

helps you determine which recorded facts are supported by sources. It can be useful in keeping track of the sources you've researched and lets you compare notes with other researchers.

Calendars

You can make a monthly calendar (fig. 10-23) that displays birthdays, death dates, and anniversaries included in your tree. Because you can choose which individuals to include, you can create a calendar for your own family or make one that celebrates your ancestors.

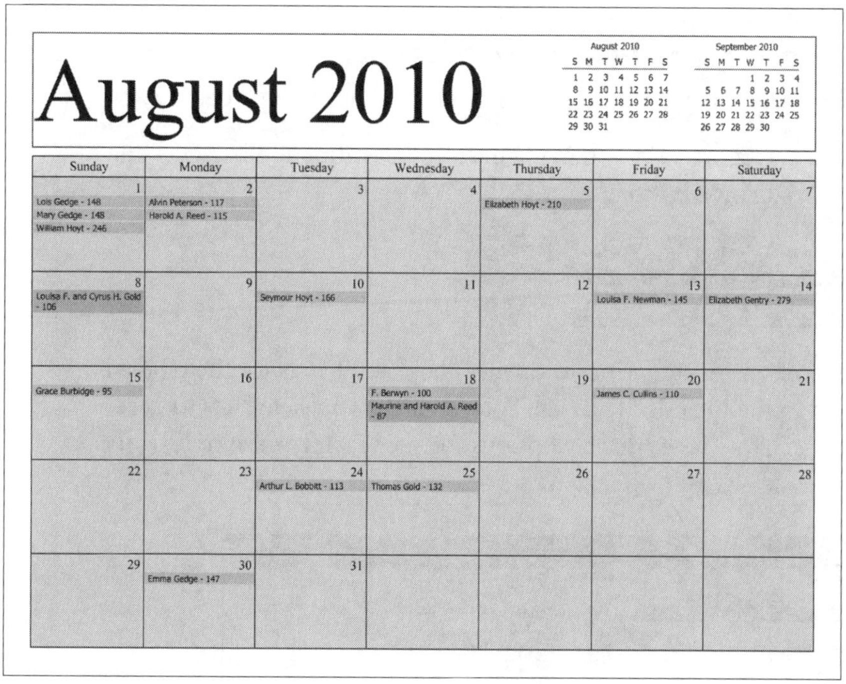

Figure 10-23

A calendar showing birth dates for all individuals.

Creating a Report

All reports are based on the last individual you were viewing in your tree. To change the primary individual in the report, click his or her name in the mini pedigree tree above the report, or click the Index of Individuals button and choose the person you want.

1. Go to the Collection tab on the Publish workspace. In **Publication Types**, click the report type you want.

2. Double-click the report icon, or select its icon and then click the **Detail** tab.

3. Use the editing panel to change the report.

Customizing a Report

You can customize the contents and format of many reports in Family Tree Maker. For example, you can determine which individuals and facts are included in the report and choose background images and text options.

Choosing Facts to Include in a Report

In some reports you can choose which facts you'd like to include.

1. Access the report you want to change. In the editing toolbar, click the **Items to include** button.

The Items to Include window opens. The default facts for the report are shown in the Included facts list. You can add and delete facts for a report and also change display options for each fact. For example, you can change the order in which a name displays.

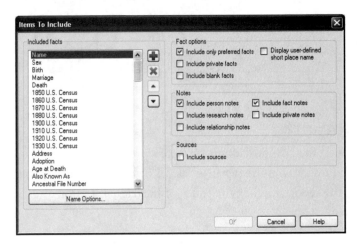

2. Do one of these options:

    • To delete a fact from a report, click the fact in the Included facts list and click the red (**X**) button.

    • To add a fact to the report, click the blue (+) button. The Select Fact window opens. Choose a fact from the list and click **OK**.

3. Choose which types of facts to include or exclude:

    • You may have multiple facts for the same event. Click **Include only preferred facts** to include only the facts designated as "preferred."

    • Click **Include private facts** to include facts designated as "private."

    • Click **Include blank facts** to include a fact field even if the fact has not been entered for an individual.

    • If you have entered shortened place names for locations, click **Display user-defined short place name** to use these locations in the report.

4. To determine a fact's format in the report, click the fact in the "Included facts" list and click the **Options** button. Then select the options you want and click **OK**.

    Note: The options for each fact vary. For example, with births, marriages, and deaths, you can include dates and locations.

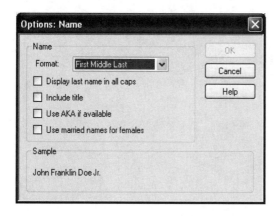

5. Choose which types of notes to include in the report:

   - Click **Include person notes** to include notes linked to individuals.

   - Click **Include research notes** to include research notes linked to individuals.

   - Click **Include relationship notes** to include person notes linked to relationships.

   - Click **Include fact notes** to include notes linked to facts.

   - Click **Include private notes** to include any note that has been designated as "private."

6. To show sources in the report, click the **Include sources** checkbox.

7. Click **OK**.

Choosing Individuals to Include in a Report

In many reports, you can choose which individuals will be included. You might want to choose a specific ancestor and only his or her descendants, or you may choose to include everyone in the tree. You can also choose individuals by picking specific criteria (for example, you may want to generate a report that shows all individuals who were born in a particular city).

1. Access the report you want to change. You can choose individuals for the report in the editing panel.

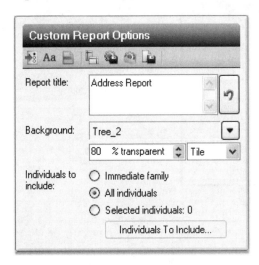

2. Do one of these options:

   - If you want to include the individual's immediate family members, click **Immediate family**.

   - If you want to include everyone in your tree in the report, click **All individuals**.

   - If you want to choose specific individuals to include in the report, click **Selected individuals**. The Filter Individuals window opens. Click a name and then click **Include** to add the person. When you're finished choosing individuals click **OK**.

Changing a Report's Title

You can edit the title that appears at the top of a report. Access the report you want to change. In the editing panel, enter a name for the report in the **Report title** field.

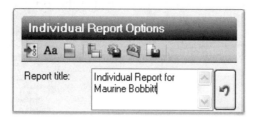

Adding a Background Image

Family Tree Maker comes with several attractive images you can use as your report's background, or you can select images stored on your computer or family pictures you've already added to your tree.

1. Access the report you want to change. In the editing panel, choose an image from the **Background** drop-down list:

   - To look for an item on your computer's hard drive, click **Browse for Image**. The Select Report Background Image window opens. Choose an image and click **Open**.

   - To choose an image you've already added to your tree, click **Select from Media Collection**. The Find Media Item window opens. Choose an image and click **OK**.

2. Choose how the background will be displayed on the report. If you want the image centered in the background, choose **Center**. If you want the image stretched to fit the entire page, choose **Stretch**. If you want a close-up of the image, choose **Zoom**. If you want a series of the same image to fill the background, choose **Tile**.

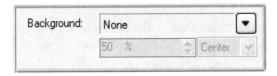

3. In the **Transparent** drop-down list, choose the intensity of the image. At 0 percent, the image will appear at its usual intensity, while a higher percentage will fade the image so the report is easier to read.

Changing the Header or Footer

You can define the headers and footers for a report (the lines of text at the top and bottom of a report).

1. Access the report you want to change. In the editing toolbar, click the **Header/Footer** button.

2. Change the header and footer options as necessary:

 • **Show report title on every page.** Click this checkbox to display a title (header) on each page of the report.

 • **Show footer.** Click this checkbox to display a footer on each page of the report. Click **Include page number** to display a page number on the left side of the footer; click **Include print date** to display the current date on the right side of the footer; click **Include print time** to display the current time next to the current date.

3. Click **OK**.

Changing Fonts

You can change the appearance of the text in reports to make it more formal, more fun, or maybe just more readable.

1. Access the report you want to change. In the editing toolbar, click the **Fonts** button.

2. In the **Items to format** list, click the text element, such as the report title, you would like to change.

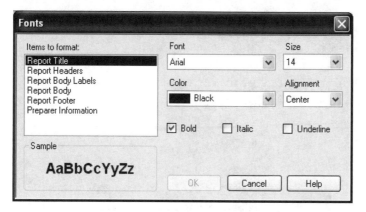

3. Choose a font from the **Font** drop-down list. You can also change the size of the text, its style, color, and alignment. The Sample box shows you how your font choices will appear in the report.

4. Click **OK** to save your changes.

Saving Reports

You can save a specific report that can be accessed in Family Tree Maker (or just its settings) or you can save a report in different file formats you can export.

Saving the Settings for a Report

After you customize a report, you can save your settings so you won't have to recreate these changes the next time you access the report. The settings you can save depend on the report, but generally include fact options, fonts, headers and footers, page layouts, and background images.

Note: You cannot save settings in one report and use them in another. For example, if you save settings in the Parentage Report, you cannot use these settings in the Kinship Report.

1. Make any necessary modifications to the report, and click the **Save settings** button in the editing toolbar.

2. A message asks if you want to use the current settings as the "preferred" settings for this report type. Click **Yes**.

TIP

If you don't want to use the settings anymore, you can quickly change back to the report's default settings. Click the **Use report settings** button in the editing toolbar. Then choose **Default settings** and click **OK**.

Saving a Specific Report

After you've modified or customized a report for an individual or family line you may want to save it. That way you can access the exact report again without having to recreate it.

1. After you have modified the report, click the **Save report** button in the editing toolbar.

2. Enter a name for the report in the **Report name** field. Be sure to use a name that will distinguish the report from others. For example, don't use generic terms like "Family Group Sheet" or "Custom Report."

3. Click **Save**.

> **TIP**
>
> To open a saved report, go to the Collection tab on the Publish workspace. In Publication Types, click **Saved Reports**. Then double-click the report you want to open.

Saving a Report as a File

You may want to save a report to a file format compatible with software other than Family Tree Maker; for example, a spreadsheet or word-processing program. These files can be easily shared with others or posted on a website.

1. Access the report you want to save.

2. Click the **Share** button above the editing panel. From the drop-down list, choose one of these options:

   - **Export to PDF.** An Adobe PDF (Portable Document Format) is useful because PDFs keep the formatting you select. That way, if you print your report or send it to a relative, the report will look exactly as you see it on your monitor. You cannot make changes to the PDF within

Family Tree Maker, and you need the Adobe Reader in order to view it. (Reader can be downloaded for free from the Adobe website.)

- **Export to CSV.** This format organizes information into fields (comma-separated values) and is meant to be imported into spreadsheet programs. Only reports that use column formats can be exported to CSV.

- **Export to RTF.** This word-processor format is based on a basic text file, but it can include information such as text style, size, and color. Also, this is a universal format, so it can be read by nearly all word processors.

- **Export to HTML.** Hypertext Markup Language is the standard language for creating and formatting Web pages.

Each format has its own export options you can choose from. After you choose a format type, you may be able to choose options such as page borders and text separators. Once you've made your selections, a file management window opens.

3. Navigate to the location you want. Then enter a name for the report in the field and click **Save**.

Printing a Report

When you are done creating and customizing a report, you may want to print it out. Family Tree Maker makes it easy to choose setup options and print a report.

1. Access the report you want to print.

2. Click the **Print** button above the editing panel. Just like printing from any other application, you can choose a printer, select the number of copies, and choose a page range.

3. Click **Print**.

Sharing a Report

Family Tree Maker lets you share reports with others—via e-mail—in a variety of formats.

Note: You must be connected to the Internet and have a desktop e-mail program to use this feature.

1. Access the report you want to e-mail.

2. Click the **Share** button above the editing panel. From the drop-down list, choose one of these options:

    *   **Send as PDF.** The Adobe PDF retains printer formatting and graphical elements so it resembles how the printed document will appear.

    *   **Send as CSV.** This format organizes information into fields (comma-separated values) and is meant to be imported into spreadsheet programs. Only reports that use column formats can be exported to CSV.

    *   **Send as RTF.** This word-processor format is based on a basic text file, but it can include information such as text style, size, and color. Also, this is a universal format, so it can be read by nearly all word processors.

    *   **Send as Image.** This option lets you create an image of the report as a bitmap, JPEG, and other image formats.

    Each format has its own export options you can choose from. After you choose a format type, you may be able to choose options such as page borders and text separators. Once you've made your selections, click **OK**. A file management window opens.

3. Navigate to the location where you want to save the report. Then enter a name for the report and click **Save**. Family Tree Maker opens a new e-mail (with the file attached) in your default e-mail program.

4. Send the e-mail as you would any other.

Chapter Eleven
Creating a Family History Book

Wouldn't you love to have a printed family history to share your family stories, photographs, maps, and research? And what could be more convenient than using the same software to organize your family history *and* create a book to tell your ancestral story?

Family Tree Maker gives you access to two publishing tools that will help you create a quality family history book that you and your family will enjoy for many years to come. The first tool is a desktop book-building feature built into the Family Tree Maker software. It's a great way to assemble a traditional genealogy using the images, facts, charts, and reports you've already entered in your tree; you can also use the text-editing features to add stories and additional information. The second tool is MyCanvas, a Web-based publishing service. It's perfect for creating scrapbooks, photo books, memorial books, and more informal family histories.

The Desktop Book-Building Tool

Family Tree Maker lets you create a family history right on your own desktop using its book-building tool. Getting started is easy because you can use the facts, photos, charts, reports, and timelines already in your file. Add some personal stories and anecdotes, and you're ready to combine all the pieces together into a real book you can share with others electronically or take to a copy shop to be printed and bound.

Starting a Family History Book

1. Go to the **Collection** tab on the Publish workspace. In **Publication Types**, click **Books**.

2. Double-click **Genealogy Book**. The Save Book window opens.

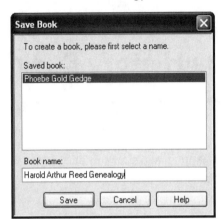

3. Enter a title for the book in the **Book name** field and click **Save**. The book opens in the text editor.

Importing a Book

If you created a book in Family Tree Maker 2006 or Version 16, you can import the book into your 2011 tree. However, because of differences between the old and new software formats, some items won't transfer over, such as images, text formatting, and NGSQ reports (placeholder pages show you where reports and charts have been left out). Before you import a book, you should make a backup of your current tree.

> Note: When you import a book, Family Tree Maker adds an explanatory page as the first item in your book. You should delete this before you share or print the book.

1. Choose **File>Import Books**. A file management window opens.

> Note: The Import Books option imports *only* books that have been created in Family Tree Maker.

2. Navigate to the Family Tree Maker (.ftw) file that contains the book you want to import and click **Open**. When the import is complete, you'll see the Success window, which shows how many books and book items were imported.

3. Click **OK**. The books are added to your Saved Books list.

4. To view your imported book, go to the **Collection** tab on the Publish workspace.

5. In **Publication Types**, click **Saved Books**.

6. Double-click the book you imported, or select its icon and then click the **Detail** tab. The book opens in the text editor.

If Family Tree Maker was unable to import an item (such as a timeline, map, or report), click on the missing item in the outline and its place-holder text will explain what has been left out—and in some cases, who the item was attached to (fig. 11-1).

> This report or chart failed to import correctly or is not currently supported in Family Tree Maker 2010.
>
> Type: BKI_TIMELINE
>
> Title: Timeline
> Root Person: James Clarence Bobbitt

Figure 11-1

A timeline that was not imported into the book.

Accessing a Saved Book

1. Go to the **Collection** tab on the Publish workspace. In **Publication Types**, click **Saved Books**.

2. Double-click the book you want to open, or select its icon and then click the **Detail** tab. The book opens in the text editor.

Setting Up a Book

When you create a book you can enter information about the author, the title, and determine the headers and footers.

1. Access the book you want to set up.

2. In the book panel toolbar, click the **Book Properties** button.

The Book Properties window opens.

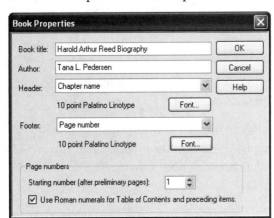

3. Change the book's properties as necessary:

- **Book title.** Enter the name of your book. This is the title that will appear in the book's headers and footers; it is not entered on the title page automatically.

- **Author.** Enter the name of the individual who wrote the book.

- **Header.** Choose a header type from the drop-down list. Headers are typically the title of a book, but you can choose to have no header, or a combination of the book title, chapter name, and page number. To change the header's font, click **Font** and choose a style and size from the drop-down list.

  Note: You can change the header for a specific page using Item Properties (see "Changing an Item's Settings" on page 203).

- **Footer.** Choose a footer type from the drop-down list. Footers are typically page numbers, but you can choose to have no footer, or a combination of the book title, chapter name, and page number. To change the footer's font, click **Font** and choose a style and size from the drop-down list.

  Note: You can change the footer for a specific page using Item Properties (see "Changing an Item's Settings" on page 203).

- **Starting number.** Choose what page you want the body of the book to start on (the front matter—title page, table of contents, dedication, etc.—will be numbered separately).

- **Use Roman numerals.** Click this checkbox to use the standard Roman numerals (i, ii, iii, iv) for the book's front matter—title page, table of contents, dedication, etc.

4. Click **OK**.

Adding Content to a Book

You can add any number of items to your family history book, including stories, photos, reports, charts, and even an automatically generated table of contents and index.

Adding Text

Don't let your family history book become a dry recitation of facts. Add interest and personality by including family stories and memories. If your grandfather immigrated to America when he was young, don't just list this fact in an individual report. Include a photo of the ship your grandfather arrived on and an excerpt from his journal that tells how he felt when he saw the Statue of Liberty for the first time.

Family Tree Maker has three options for entering text: you can manually type text, import text from another text file or document, or use Smart Stories to extract facts, sources, and notes you've already entered in your tree (for more information on Smart Stories, see page 47).

Adding a Text Item

Before you can add stories you'll need to add a text item to your book. A text item is basically a blank sheet of paper that you open in the book text-editor. Creating one is much like opening a new document in a word-processing program. You can use it to create everything from an entire chapter to a simple page with a photo and a caption.

1. Access the book you want to add a text item to. In the book panel toolbar, click the **Add Book Item** (+) button.

The Add Book Item window opens.

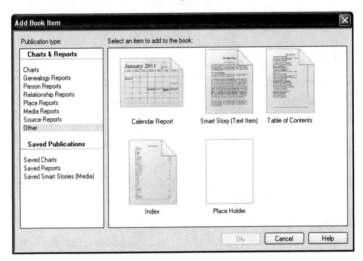

2. In the Add Book Item window, click **Other**. Then double-click **Text Item**, or select its icon and then click **OK**. A blank page opens in the text editor.

Entering Text Manually

You can use the text editor to write your own family narratives.

1. Access the text item you want to add text to by clicking its name in the book panel.

2. Place your cursor where you want the text to begin. Then type the text you want to add.

Importing Text from Another Document

If you've already written your book in another text program, you don't have to re-type your text or copy and paste sections into Family Tree Maker. You can import the entire document at once—without losing formatting.

1. Access the text item you want to import text into by clicking its name in the book panel.

2. Place your cursor where you want the text to begin. In the text editor, choose **File>Open**. A file management window opens.

3. Navigate to the document you want to import and click **Open**. The document opens in the text editor.

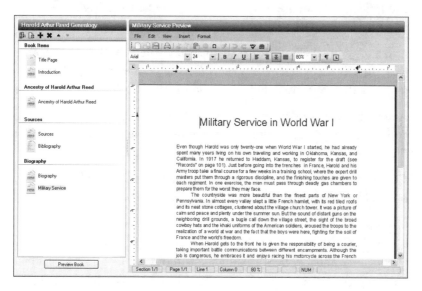

Formatting Text

The text formatting options available in a Family Tree Maker book are similar to those in any word processing program. You can change fonts, text size, alignment, tabs, indents, and more.

1. Access the text item you want to add formatting to by clicking its name in the book panel.

2. Format the text using these options:

   - **Change the font color, size, or style.** Select the text you want to change. Click **Format>Character**. The Font window opens. Make the necessary changes and click **OK**.

   - **Change the amount of space between lines of text.** Select the paragraph that has line spacing you want to change. Click **Format>Paragraph**. On the Formatting and Indents tab, choose a spacing option from the **Line spacing** drop-down list. Click **OK**.

   - **Change the indent of a paragraph.** Select the paragraph you want to change the indent for. Click **Format>Paragraph**. On the Formatting and Indents tab, choose new indents from the **Left** and **Right** drop-down lists. Click **OK**.

   - **Add a page break.** Place your cursor where you want the page break to occur. Click **Format>Paragraph**. On the Frame and Page Breaks tab, click the **Page break before** checkbox. Click **OK**.

   - **Add a frame around a paragraph.** Select the paragraph you want to add a frame to. Click **Format>Paragraph**. On the Frame and Page Breaks tab, choose the type of frame you want. Click **OK**.

   - **Change the document's tabs.** Click **Format>Tabs**. The Tabs window opens. Make the necessary changes and click **OK**.

Adding Images

What family history book would be complete without family photos, personal correspondence, record images, and maps? Family Tree Maker lets you add any image you've included in your family tree to your book. You can also add images you've stored elsewhere on your computer that you don't necessarily want to keep in your family tree—for example, clip art embellishments.

1. Access the text item you want to add an image to by clicking its name in the book panel.

   Note: In the book-building tool you cannot wrap text around images. If you don't want the image to be in-line with the text, you may want to add space before and after the object.

2.   Place your cursor where you want the image to appear.

3.   Do one of these options:

*   To add an image you've uploaded to Family Tree Maker, choose **Insert>Image from Media Collection**. The Find Media Item window opens. Select the image and click **OK**.

*   To add an image from your computer, choose **Insert>Image from File**. Navigate to the image you want and click **Open**.

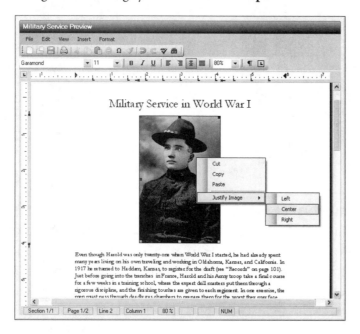

Note: You can also add images linked to individuals by clicking the Media button on the Smart Stories toolbar (for more information see page 51). Select the image you want and drag it to your document.

4.   To align the image, right-click it. Then choose "Left," "Center," or "Right" from the **Justify Image** drop-down list. You can also move the image by dragging it to a new location.

5. If you need to resize an image, click on the image. Then drag one of the square handles to change the size. To maintain the image's proportions, drag the image from one of the corners.

Adding a Chart or Report

You can add as many charts and reports to a book as you'd like. Make sure you choose ones that are appropriate for your audience. For example, you may want to share more personal and informal trees and reports in a book meant for your children, but you'll want to remove information about living relatives if you plan on sharing your book with other genealogists.

1. Access the book you want to add a chart or report to.

2. In the book panel toolbar, click the **Add Book Item** (+) button.

3. In the Add Book Item window click the category for the chart or report you want to use. Then double-click the chart/report, or select its icon and click **OK**.

> **TIP**
>
> You can also click **Saved Charts** or **Saved Reports** to use documents you've already created.

The chart or report opens. You can use the editing panel to change the chart or report just as you would if you were creating it outside of the book (for instructions on customizing charts and reports, see chapters 9 and 10).

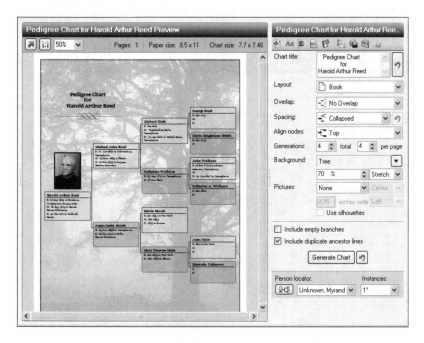

Adding a Placeholder

If you want to incorporate a story, chart, or photo from outside Family Tree Maker, you can use a placeholder to reserve a specific number of pages until you're ready to add the information.

1. Access the book you want to add a placeholder to.

2. In the book panel toolbar, click the **Add Book Item** (+) button.

3. In the Add Book Item window, click **Other**. Then double-click **Place Holder**, or select its icon and then click **OK**.

4. Choose the number of pages you want to reserve from the **Number of pages** field.

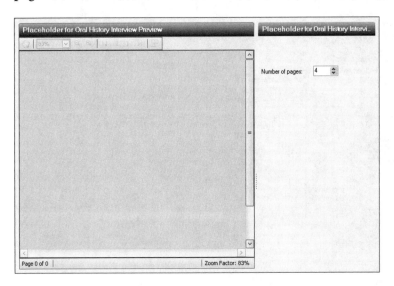

> ### TIP
> Give the placeholder a descriptive name so you don't forget what you were going to use it for. You can change its name by clicking the Book Item Properties button in the book panel toolbar.

Creating a Table of Contents

Family Tree Maker can automatically generate a table of contents for your book. If you make changes to your book (such as adding a new chart or moving a text item) Family Tree Maker will update the table of contents and its page numbers to reflect the changes.

> Note: The table of contents is automatically added after the title page. You can change the order of the front matter—table of contents, dedication, preface, etc.—but you cannot move the table of contents out of the front matter.

1. Access the book you want to add a table of contents to.

2. In the book panel toolbar, click the **Add Book Item** (+) button.

3. In the Add Book Item window, click **Other**. Then double-click **Table of Contents**, or select its icon and then click **OK**. The table of contents opens.

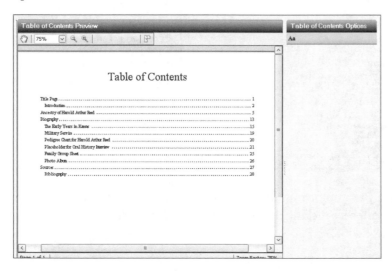

Although you cannot directly edit the table of contents, you can customize the text's font, size, and color by clicking the Fonts button under the "Table of Contents Options" heading.

Creating an Index of Individuals

Family Tree Maker can automatically generate an index that lists all the individuals included in the book's reports and charts (names mentioned in text items will *not* be included). If you make changes to your book (such as adding a new chart) Family Tree Maker will update the index to reflect the change.

Note: The index cannot be moved; it must be the last item in your book.

1. Access the book you want to add an index to.

2. In the book panel toolbar, click the **Add Book Item** (+) button.

3. In the Add Book Item window, click **Other**. Then double-click **Index**, or select its icon and then click **OK**. The index opens.

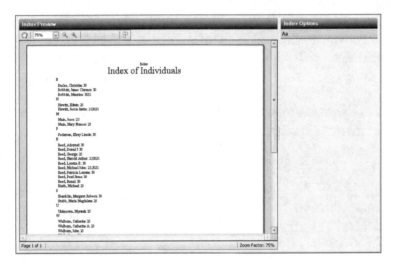

Although you cannot edit the index, you can customize the text's font, size, and color by clicking the Fonts button under the "Index Options" heading.

Organizing a Book

As your book grows, you may find that it has changed from the project you originally envisioned and that you need to make some adjustments. Perhaps you've uncovered additional records and photos and you want to rearrange a couple of chapters to include them. Or maybe you decided that it wasn't necessary to include a Research Note report. Family Tree Maker makes it easy to change titles, rearrange the order of how things appear in your book, or even delete sections you don't need.

Changing an Item's Settings

A Family Tree Maker book is made up of a variety of different book items: text items, charts, reports, etc. You can change settings for each book item.

1. Access the book you want to change. Then access the item you want to change.

2. In the book panel toolbar, click the **Book Item Properties** button.

The Item Properties window opens.

3. Change the item's settings using these options:

- **Change the item's title.** Enter a title in the **Item name** field. This is the title that will appear in the book's table of contents and this item's headers and footers.

- **Make this item start a new chapter.** Click the **This item begins a chapter** checkbox.

- **Make the first page of this item start on an odd-numbered (right-facing) page.** Click the **Start this item on an odd numbered page** checkbox. Typically each chapter starts on an odd-numbered page.

- **Prevent a page number from appearing on the first page of an item.** Click the **Do not print page number on the first page** checkbox. Typically chapter openers do not include a page number. You may also want to use this option for reports, charts, and full-page images.

- **Display headers in the item.** Click the **Include the header in this item** checkbox.

- **Display footers in the item.** Click the **Include the footer in this item** checkbox.

4. Click **OK**.

Rearranging Book Items

The book panel shows you all the items you've included in a book. The order in which they're displayed in this outline is the order in which they'll print. You can change this order at any time.

1. Access the book you want to change. Then click on the item you want to move in the book panel.

2. To change an item's order in the outline, select the item. Then click the **Move Up** and **Move Down** buttons in the book editing toolbar. (You can also drag items to the desired location.)

Deleting a Book Item

If you decide you don't want a text item, report, or chart you've included in your book, you can delete it.

1. Access the book you want to delete an item from. Then click on the item in the book panel.

2. Click the **Delete Book Item** button.

Printing a Book at Home

When you are done creating your book, you can make copies on your home printer.

> Note: If you want to see what your book will look like when it is printed, click the **Preview Book** button below the book outline.

1. Access the book you want to print. Then click the **Print** button below the main toolbar.

   The Print window opens. Just like printing from any other application, you can choose a printer, select the number of copies to print, and choose a page range.

2. Click **Print**.

Exporting a Book

You can export your book as a PDF and take it to a copy shop to be printed and professionally bound or e-mail it to family members.

1. Access the book you want to export. Then click the **Share** button below the main toolbar.

2. Choose **Export to PDF** from the drop-down list. The PDF Export Options window opens.

3. Change format options as necessary and click **OK**. A file management window opens; click **OK** again.

MyCanvas

MyCanvas is a Web-based publishing program and printing service provided by Ancestry.com that you can use to create a family history book using your Family Tree Maker tree.

After you upload your tree to Ancestry.com, MyCanvas gets you started by automatically generating pages (pedigree trees, family group sheets, and even timelines) based on information in your tree. You can then use its intuitive features to modify these pages by adding photos, stories, historical records, and more. You can also add more pages to your book or delete pages you don't like. When you're finished, you can have your book professionally printed and bound—an heirloom to be enjoyed and shared for years to come.

Note: This section explains how to upload your Family Tree Maker tree to MyCanvas, the Ancestry publishing tool; it does not explain how to use its features. To learn more about the tool, go to <www.ancestry.com> and click the Publish button on the main toolbar. On the left side of the window under "Support," click **Help**. You'll find tips and tricks for using the tool, and even videos.

Creating a MyCanvas Book

When you're ready to create a MyCanvas book, you will upload your tree to MyCanvas and create a project. You can choose which individuals you want to include in your projects. That way, you can create as many books as you'd like—maybe even one book for each branch of your family.

Note: You must be a registered user or have a subscription to Ancestry.com to upload your tree. You must also be connected to the Internet to use this feature.

Uploading Your Tree to Ancestry.com

1. Go to the **Collection** tab on the Publish workspace.
2. In **Publication Types**, click **Books**.

3. Double-click **Create a Professionally Printed Book Online**. The Upload to MyCanvas window opens.

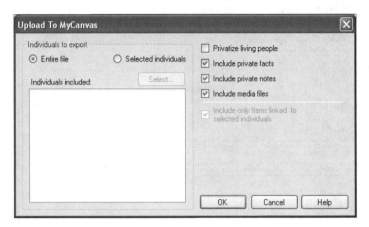

You can choose which individuals are included in the tree you're uploading.

4. Do one of these options:

   - If you want to include all the individuals in your tree, click **Entire file**.

   - If you want to choose only a few specific individuals to include in the tree, click **Selected individuals**. The Filter Individuals window will open. Click a name and then click **Include** to add the person. When you're finished choosing individuals, click **OK**.

5. If you're going to be sharing your book with people other than immediate family members, you might want to leave out private facts and notes. To do so, make sure the **Include private facts** and **Include private notes** checkboxes are not selected.

6. If you want media items linked to a tree to be uploaded to your book project, click the **Include media files** checkbox.

7. Click **OK**. If necessary, log in to your Ancestry.com account.

   While the tree is being uploaded, you'll see the Upload to MyCanvas window, which shows the number of individuals, families, etc. that are being uploaded.

A browser window opens. You will complete a few short fields to finish the tree upload; then your family information will be transferred to the MyCanvas publishing tool.

8. Enter a name for your tree in the **Tree Name** field.

9. If you want your tree to be viewable to all Ancestry members, click the **Allow others to see my tree** checkbox.

   Note: If you choose to keep your tree private, Ancestry members can still see names, birth dates, and birthplaces from your tree in search results. However, if they want to see the full tree or any attached photos and records, they will have to use the Ancestry Connection Service to contact you. Then you can choose to give them access to your tree or not.

10. Click the checkbox to accept the submission agreement.

11. Click **Upload**. The MyCanvas window opens. Continue with the next task, "Setting Up a MyCanvas Book."

Setting Up a MyCanvas Book

1. Click the book icon for the type of book you want to create (standard, combination, or descendant). Click the "Details and Cover Options" link to see more information about each book type.

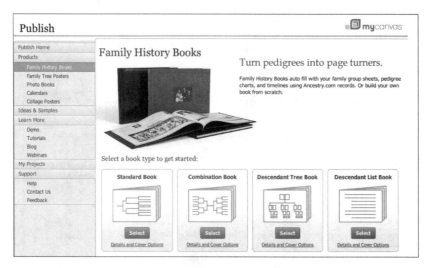

You can now choose a few options for your book.

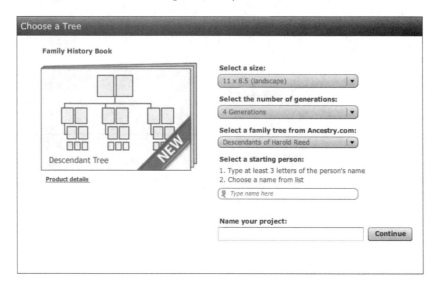

2. Choose the book's size and the number of generations included.

3. Choose the family tree you want to use. (Because you just uploaded your tree from Family Tree Maker, this should be the default tree selected.)

4. Start typing the name of the individual you want to be the "root" person in your tree. The tool will try to recognize the name as you enter it. To use the suggested name, click it in the drop-down list.

5. Enter a name for your project in the **Name your project** field.

6. Click **Continue**. Your book project opens.

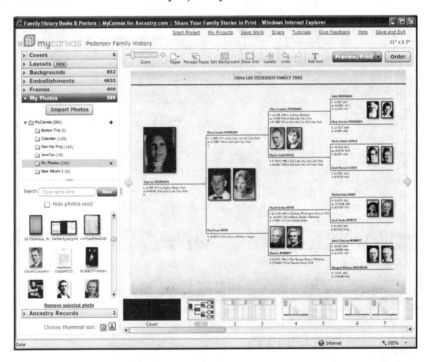

You can now use the MyCanvas publishing tool to create your book. Your book project is saved automatically every five minutes; however, make sure you save your project before you close the tool.

Accessing a MyCanvas Book

Once you've created a MyCanvas book, whether through this software or Ancestry.com, it's easy to access it from Family Tree Maker.

Note: You must be connected to the Internet to access a MyCanvas book.

1. Go to the **Collection** tab on the Publish workspace.

2. In **Publication Types**, click **Books**. Then double-click **Go to Existing Online Projects**. A Web browser opens, and the My Projects page is displayed.

3. In the center of the window, you will see thumbnail images of your projects. When you find the project you want to open, click its thumbnail. The MyCanvas publishing tool opens in a new window.

How Does MyCanvas Work?

MyCanvas is one of the many offerings from Ancestry.com—the parent company of Family Tree Maker. MyCanvas is a Web-based tool that allows you to create your own family history books, photo albums, family tree posters, and more. If you have already created a family tree using Ancestry.com or Family Tree Maker, you can use this tree for your project and let MyCanvas start the work for you. The information in your tree will be placed in professionally designed templates. You can leave the pages "as is" or use the interactive tools to add additional photographs, embellishments, and text.

When you complete your book, you may want to print some pages on your desktop printer. Keep in mind, if you choose to print at home, pages will have a low resolution (meaning text and images won't look sharp), and if you have lots of colorful photographs and backgrounds, you can go through quite a bit of ink or toner. Through MyCanvas, you can buy a high-resolution copy of your book and have it printed, professionally bound, and sent to your door.

Each unique book you create preserves your heritage and is an exciting way to share your discoveries with family and friends. And these books also make great gifts for anniversaries, birthdays, and reunions.

Part Four

Managing Your Trees

Chapter Twelve
Working with Trees

In chapter 3 you learned how to create and import new trees. This chapter will explain the many tools Family Tree Maker has to help you manage, share, and protect your trees.

Managing Your Trees

This section explains the basic tasks you'll need to know to manage your trees effectively whether you're working on one comprehensive tree or multiple trees.

Opening a Tree

When you launch Family Tree Maker, it automatically opens the last tree you were working in. You can switch to a different tree when necessary.

Note: If you try to open a GEDCOM, a file from a previous version of Family Tree Maker, or a file from another genealogical program, the software automatically opens the New Tree tab. You can't open the file; you will need to import it (for instructions, see "Importing a Tree" on page 26).

1. Click the **Plan** button on the main toolbar. On the right side of the window you'll see trees you've recently worked on.

2. Do one of these options:

    •   If the tree you want to open is in the list, double-click its name, or highlight the tree and click **Options>Open Tree**.

    •   If the tree you want to open isn't in the list, you can look for the file on your hard drive. Click **Options>Browse**. A file management window opens. Navigate to the tree you want and click **Open**.

Renaming a Tree

You can change the name of a tree at any time.

1. Click the **Plan** button on the main toolbar.

2. In the Trees section, highlight a tree and click **Options>Rename Tree**.

3. Enter a new name for the tree and click **OK**.

Viewing Information About a Tree

The Current Tree tab on the Plan workspace contains a summary about the tree you're working on. You can view information about the computer file, such as its size and the last day you backed up your data. You can also view information about the people in your tree, for example, the number of marriages, individuals, surnames, and sources in your tree.

1. Go to the **Current Tree** tab on the Plan workspace. A basic summary of your file appears at the top of the tab.

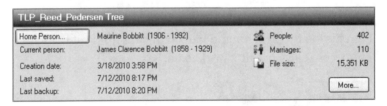

2. To see additional statistics about your tree, click the **More** button. The File Statistics window opens.

Deleting a Tree

If necessary, you can delete an entire tree at once.

1. Click the **Plan** button on the main toolbar.

2. In the Trees section, highlight a tree and click **Options>Delete Tree**.

3. If you want to delete the media files that are linked to the tree, click **Move selected linked files** and select the files you'd like to delete. Then click **OK**.

Using Privacy Mode

Your tree probably contains personal information about family members who are still living or even confidential details about you. Before you export a family history book or print a family tree chart to share with others, you might want to "privatize" your tree. In privacy mode information about living individuals, such as dates and facts, will not be displayed. Be aware that you will not be able to edit the tree or add additional information until you turn off privacy mode.

1. Click **File>Privatize File**. You can tell when a tree is in privacy mode because the word "Privatized" appears in the window's title bar and a checkmark appears next to the Privatize File option in the File menu.

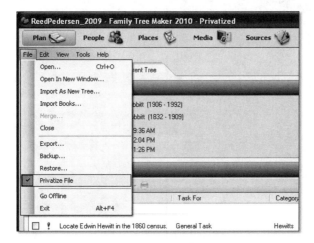

2. When you want to continue working in your tree, turn off privacy mode by clicking **File>Privatize File** again.

Exporting a Tree File

If you want to share your family tree with someone, you can export all or part of a file as a GEDCOM—the standard file format used to transfer data between different genealogy software. You can also export your tree as a Family Tree Maker file; however, it will be compatible only with Family Tree Maker 2011.

Note: While Family Tree Maker lets you add digital images, sound, and videos to your tree, these items are not included if you export to a GEDCOM.

GEDCOM

Because your great-aunt may not use the same software that you use, you'll need to share your family history in a file format that anyone can open. That format is GEDCOM. GEDCOM stands for GEnealogical Data COMmunications; it allows genealogy files to be opened in any genealogy software program. GEDCOMs are compatible with Macs and PCs.

1. Click **File>Export**. The Export window opens.

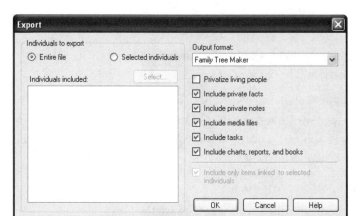

2. Do one of these options:

   • If you want to export the entire tree, click **Entire file**.

   • If you want to choose specific individuals to include in the file, click **Selected individuals**. The Filter Individuals window will open. Click a name and then click **Include** to add the person. When you're finished choosing individuals, click **OK**.

3. Choose "GEDCOM" or "Family Tree Maker" from the **Output format** drop-down list.

4. Choose the information you want included in the export file:

   • **Privatize living people.** Click this checkbox if you do not want to include information about individuals who are still living. Names and relationships will be included, but facts and shared facts will not be exported.

   • **Include private facts.** Click this checkbox to export facts you have designated as private.

   • **Include private notes.** Click this checkbox to export notes you have designated as private.

   • **Include media files.** Click this checkbox to export all media files that are linked to the tree.

   Note: This option is not available for GEDCOMs.

- **Include tasks.** Click this checkbox to export tasks you've added to your Research To-Do list.

  Note: This option is not available for GEDCOMs.

- **Include charts, reports, and books.** Click this checkbox to export charts, reports, and books you've saved.

  Note: This option is not available for GEDCOMs.

- **Include only items linked to selected individuals.** Click this checkbox to export *only* tasks, notes, and media items that are linked to the individuals you're exporting.

5. Click **OK**. An export window opens.

6. Navigate to the location where you want to save the file.

   Note: Family Tree Maker automatically names the exported file with the same name as the original tree. If you want to use a different name, you can change it.

7. Click **Save**. A message tells you when your file has been exported successfully.

Storage Types

If you are using floppy disks, use a new set each time or alternate between two sets. Since floppy disks don't hold much data, you may need several, depending on the size of your file. If you have a large tree, it's better to back up your files to a larger medium such as a CD-ROM (an optical medium, more stable than floppies) or DVD. Recordable CDs and DVDs are quite inexpensive and can hold much larger files.

When you are finished, store the floppy disks or CDs with your family history data in a separate location from your hard drive to protect the information in case of fire or flood.

Backing Up Tree Files

Your family trees are important; not only do they contain your family's history, but they also represent hours of your hard work. Unfortunately, computer files are vulnerable and can be corrupted by viruses or accidentally deleted or destroyed. You can preserve your family history through regular backups of your tree files. For example, you can back up your trees to a CD every month and archive the CD. Then, if your original tree is damaged or you want to revert to a previous copy, you can restore it from the backup.

> Note: You can have Family Tree Maker automatically back up a tree every time you exit the program. To do this, click **Tools>Options** and make sure the **Automatically backup family file** checkbox is selected.

Backing Up a File

1. Make sure the tree you want to back up is open and click **File>Backup**. The Backup window opens.

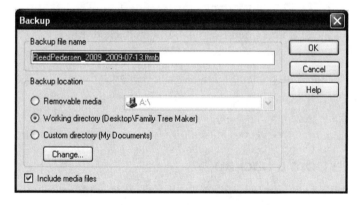

2. If you want a new name to distinguish your backup file from your original tree, enter a new name for the tree in the **Backup file name** field. For example, if you back up your trees to the same rewriteable CD every time, and this backup file has the same name as the file that is already on the CD, then this backup will write over the original file.

3. Choose one of these backup locations:

   • **Floppy disk.** Click **Removable Media**. In the drop-down list, choose your floppy disk drive.

      Note: If you are backing up a large file, Family Tree Maker will ask you to insert new diskettes as needed. When the backup requires multiple diskettes, be sure to label them in the order in which they are created.

   • **CD, DVD, or flash drive.** Click **Removable Media**. In the drop-down list, choose your CD-ROM drive, DVD drive, or flash drive.

      Note: The first time you back up a file to a CD-ROM, you may get a message asking you to install a driver—this message will appear only once.

   • **Hard drive.** Click **Working Directory** to save your file to the directory where your current tree is saved on your hard drive; click **Custom directory** to choose a new location on your hard drive.

4. Click **Include media files** to back up all media files in the tree.

5. Click **OK**. A message tells you when the file has been backed up successfully.

   Note: Backup files cannot be exchanged between genealogy software programs like GEDCOMs can. They can only be opened with the version of Family Tree Maker in which they were created.

Restoring a File from a Backup

If you need to use your backup file as your working tree, you can restore it when necessary.

1. Disable any anti-virus software you may be using.

2. If your backup file has been copied to a CD or other removable media, copy it back to your hard drive.

3. Click **File>Restore**. A file management window opens.

4. Navigate to the backup file you want to restore and click **Open**.

Note: You can identify a backup file by looking at its file extension (the letters after the file name). Family Tree Maker backup files use the .ftmb extension.

The tree will open. Any data you entered in the original tree since you created this backup will not be included.

Note: Don't forget to reenable your anti-virus software.

Compressing a Tree File

As you work in your trees you will add and delete quite a bit of data. However, even when data has been removed from a tree, the file may still be large. You should compress your tree files periodically to optimize performance, remove unnecessary items, and reindex the file.

1. Click **Tools**>**Compact File**. The Compact File window opens.

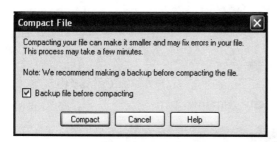

2. If you want to back up your file before you compress it, click the **Back up file before compacting** checkbox (recommended).

3. Click **Compact**. If you have chosen to back up your file, the Backup window opens. Change any options as necessary and click **OK**.

4. When Family Tree Maker is finished, a message shows how much the file size was reduced. Click **OK**.

Because file compression happens behind the scenes, you won't see any changes to your tree, but you should notice better performance and a smaller overall file size.

Uploading a Tree to Ancestry.com

Chapter 3 explained how to start a new tree using an existing tree on Ancestry.com. Family Tree Maker also lets you upload a tree to Ancestry.com. It's easy, free, and because your tree is online, it can be shared with family around the world.

Ancestry.com and Family Tree Maker use different formats for their trees so some information in your tree may not transfer as you'd expect. Here's a list of the tree elements that will be uploaded:

- Dates, Places, Names (except suffixes)
- Notes (but not formatting)
- Stories attached to individuals
- Basic sources and source citations
- Media items attached to individuals (images and documents only)

    Note: To upload a tree to Ancestry.com, you do not have to be a subscriber, but you must register your copy of Family Tree Maker and have Internet access.

1. Open the tree you want to upload to Ancestry.com.

2. Click the **Share** button on the main toolbar and choose **Upload to Ancestry**. The Upload to Ancestry window opens.

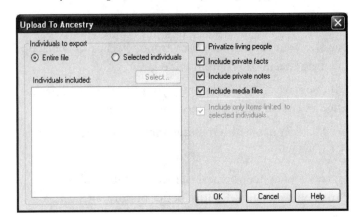

3. Do one of these options:

    • If you want to export the entire tree, click **Entire file**.

    • If you want to choose only a few specific individuals to include in the file, click **Selected individuals**. The Filter Individuals window will open. Click a name and then click **Include** to add the person. When you're finished choosing individuals, click **OK**.

4. Choose the information you want included in your Ancestry tree:

    • **Privatize living people.** Click this checkbox if you do not want to include information about individuals who are still living. Names will be replaced with the word "Living." Relationships will be included, but facts and shared facts will not be uploaded.

    • **Include private facts.** Click this checkbox to upload facts you have designated as private.

    • **Include private notes.** Click this checkbox to upload notes you have designated as private.

    • **Include media files.** Click this checkbox to upload media files that are linked to individuals.

5. Click **OK**. While the tree is being uploaded, you'll see the Upload to Ancestry window, which shows the number of individuals, families, etc. that are being uploaded. A browser window opens.

6. Enter a name for your tree in the **Tree Name** field. If you want your tree to be viewable to all Ancestry members, click the **Allow others to see my tree** checkbox.

   Note: If you choose to keep your tree private, Ancestry members can still see names, birth dates, and birthplaces from your tree in search results. However, if they want to see the full tree or any attached photos and records, they will have to use the Ancestry Connection Service to contact you. Then you can choose to give them access to your tree or not.

7. Click the checkbox to accept the submission agreement and click **Upload**. The tree opens.

Chapter Thirteen
Tools and Preferences

Using Family Tree Maker Tools

While entering information about your family in a tree, you may need some extra help calculating approximate birth dates, understanding how individuals are related to each other, or creating a Research To-do List. Family Tree Maker has several calculators and tools to help you with these tasks and more.

Soundex Calculator

Soundex is a term familiar to most family historians. Soundex is a coding system that was used by the government to create indices of U.S. census records (and some passenger lists) based on how a surname sounds rather than how it is spelled. This was done to accommodate potential spelling and transcription errors. For example, "Smith" may be spelled "Smythe," "Smithe," or "Smyth." Using Soundex, these "Smith" examples are all identified by the same Soundex code (S530). Family Tree Maker can determine the Soundex code for any surname. You can use this information to find other surnames that use that same code and then search for ancestors using all surname variations.

Click **Tools>Soundex Calculator**. Enter a surname in the **Name** field, or click **Index** to select the name of someone in your tree.

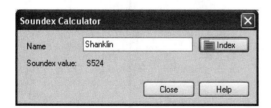

The Soundex number beneath the Name field changes automatically as you enter information in the field.

Relationship Calculator

The Relationship Calculator helps you identify the relationship between any two individuals in your tree, shows an individual's nearest common relatives, and gives his or her canon and civil numbers.

> Note: Canon and civil numbers indicate the degree of relationship between individuals. Canon laws (used in the United States) measure the number of steps back to a common ancestor. Civil degree measures the total number of steps from one family member to another.

1. Click **Tools>Relationship Calculator**. In the first field, you will see the name of your home person. In the second field, you will see the name of the individual who is the focus of your tree currently.

2. To change the individuals whose relationship you are calculating, click the **Person from people index** button next to a name (the button with an index card). In the Index of Individuals window, select a new person and click **OK**.

   The individuals' relationship is listed in the "Relationship" section. If they have multiple connections (for example when cousins marry), you can click the drop-down list to see each relationship. You can also see how the individuals are related in the "Path" section.

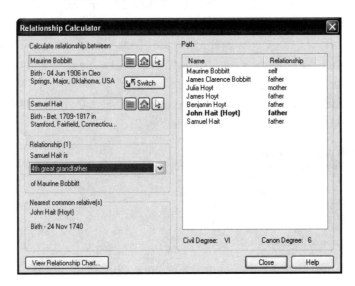

Date Calculator

You can use the Date Calculator to calculate an individual's birth year, his or her age at the time of a specific event, or the date of an event.

Calculating a Birth Date

If you know the date your grandmother was married and you know how old she was when she got married, you can determine approximately the year she was born.

1. Click **Tools>Date Calculator**. The Date Calculator opens.

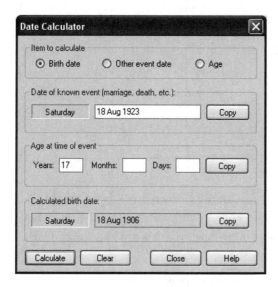

2. Click **Birth date**. Enter a date in the **Date of known event** field (in this example it would be the marriage date). Enter the individual's age in the **Age at time of event** field (in this example it would be her approximate age on the date of her marriage).

3. Click **Calculate**. The calculated birth date appears.

Calculating the Date of a Specific Event

If you know your mother's birth date and her age when she was married, you can determine approximately which year she was married.

1. Click **Tools>Date Calculator**. The Date Calculator opens.

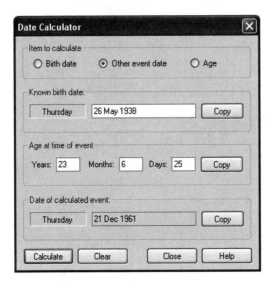

2. Click **Other event date**. Enter a date in the **Known birth date** field (in this example it would be your mother's birth date). Enter the individual's age in the **Age at time of event** field (in this example it would be her approximate age at the time of her marriage).

3. Click **Calculate**. The calculated event date appears.

Calculating an Individual's Age on a Specific Date

If you know when your great-aunt was born and you know the year she was married, you can figure out her approximate age when she was married.

1. Click **Tools**>**Date Calculator**. The Date Calculator opens.

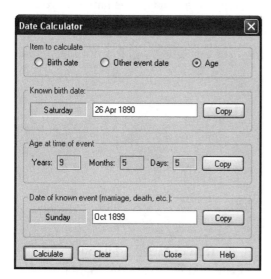

2. Click **Age**. Enter a date in the **Known birth date** field (in this example it would be your great-aunt's birth date). Enter a date in the **Date of known event** field (in this example it would be her wedding day).

3. Click **Calculate**. The calculated age of the individual appears.

Convert Names Tool

If you import another person's genealogy file into your tree, you may find that each file has recorded names differently; for example, your surnames may be capitalized while they may have capitalized only the first letter in their surnames. You can use the Convert Names tool to format all the names in your tree consistently.

1. Click **Tools>Convert Names**. The Convert Names window opens.

2. To capitalize the first letter in each name, click **First Middle Surname**. To capitalize the first letter of the first and middle names and capitalize the entire surname, click **First Middle SURNAME**.

3. Click **OK**.

Find Individual Tool

You can use any of the facts in your tree (such as occupation, immigration, or burial) to locate either a specific individual or a group of individuals who fit specific criteria. For example, you can do a search for everyone in your tree that lived in Illinois at the time of the 1850 census. Or, you might find out which individuals are all buried in the same cemetery.

> Note: The Find Individual tool searches Place and Description fields; information contained in a fact's Date field cannot be searched.

1. Click **Edit>Find Individual.** The Find Individual window opens.

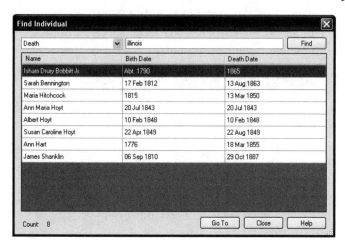

2. Choose the type of fact you want to search from the drop-down list. Then enter your search term in the next field and click **Find**.

3. If you want to access an individual's information, click his or her name in the search results and click **Go To**.

Automatic Reference Numbers

Some family historians use reference numbers to identify individuals in their trees, particularly if a tree contains individuals with duplicate names. Family Tree Maker can assign reference numbers to individuals (Person ID), relation- ships (Relationship ID), or both.

> Note: If you have already entered reference numbers manually, Family Tree Maker will not overwrite them.

1. Click **Tools>Options.** Then click the **References** tab.

2. Click **Use individual reference numbers** to choose how Family Tree Maker assigns reference numbers to individuals. Click **Use relationship reference numbers** to choose how Family Tree Maker assigns reference numbers to relationships.

Click **Numbers only** to assign numbers, starting with 1. Click **Prefix** to add a prefix before the number (you can enter numbers, letters, and/or symbols). Click **Numbers plus suffix** to add a suffix after the number (you can enter numbers, letters, and/or symbols).

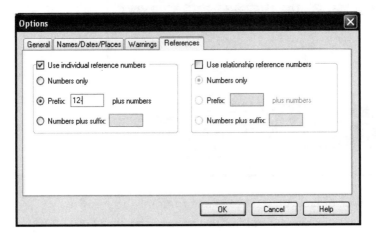

3. Click **OK**.

Research To-Do List

Whether you are a new user or an experienced family historian, the To-Do list can help you keep track of the research you've already done and let you create tasks for the next steps you need to take. You can add research tasks for specific individuals or general tasks for your entire tree; tasks can be as simple as sending an e-mail to a cousin or as complicated as locating an entire branch of your family in the 1930 census.

Creating a To-Do Task

When you create a task, you can choose the priority of the task, the category it fits in, and its due date.

Note: This section explains how to add tasks for specific individuals. You can also add tasks to the tree's To-Do list on the Current Tree tab on the Plan workspace.

1. Go to the **Person** tab for a specific individual (on the People workspace). Click the **Tasks** tab.

2. Click the **New** button in the Tasks toolbar. The Add Task window opens.

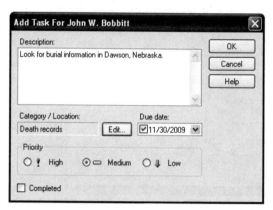

3. Enter the to-do task in the **Description** field. For example, enter "Look for burial information in Dawson, Nebraska."

4. Click **Edit** to choose a category for the task. The Category/Location window opens. Choose a category or create a category and click **OK**. (For more information, see the next task, "Creating Task Categories.")

5. Choose a deadline date for the task from the **Due date** drop-down list. Then choose a priority for the task. (Assign a high priority to the tasks you want to accomplish first.) When you're finished click **OK**.

> **TIP**
> You can print the task list for this individual by clicking the Print button on the Tasks toolbar. To print a list of all tasks in your Tree, use the Task List report on the Publish workspace.

Creating Task Categories

Each task you create can be assigned to a category. Categories can be helpful when you want to sort your To-Do list or simply for choosing tasks to work on. Because everyone conducts research a little differently, you can create category topics that are useful for you. Examples of categories are records such as census or vital, or surnames, such as the Smiths and the Lees.

1. Go to the **Current Tree** tab on the Plan workspace. In the Tasks section, you can see your current Research To-Do list.

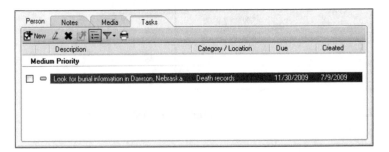

2. Click **New**. The Add Task window opens. Click **Edit**. The Category/Location window opens, showing all the currently available categories.

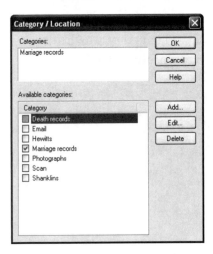

3. Click **Add**. The Add Category Name window opens.

4. Enter a name in the **Category name** field and click **OK**. Click **OK** again.

Marking a Task as Complete

When you finish a task on your To-Do list, you'll want to mark it as complete. Go to the **Current Tree** tab on the Plan workspace. In the Tasks section, click the checkbox next to the task.

> **TIP**
>
> To delete a To-Do task, click the task name and click the red (X) button in the tasks toolbar.

Sorting the To-Do List

The Research To-Do list is your road map to the research you have completed and the tasks you still have to do. You can filter the list in various ways. For example, you can sort the list to show which tasks are done or are still pending.

1. Go to the **Current Tree** tab on the Plan workspace.

2. In the Tasks section, click the **Filter tasks** button and choose one of these options from the drop-down list:

    *   To show every task you've entered, choose **Show All Tasks**.

    *   To show tasks that haven't been completed yet, choose **Show Uncompleted Tasks**.

    *   To show tasks that belong to a specific category, choose **Filter by Task Categories**.

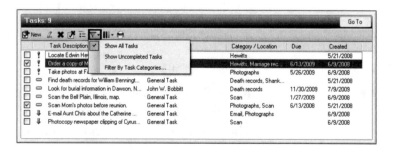

237

Note: You can also change the information that displays for each task (such as due date) by showing or hiding columns. Click the **Show/Hide columns** button in the Tasks toolbar. Then, from the drop-down list, select or deselect specific columns.

Setting Up Preferences

Family Tree Maker is a powerful program that offers you many features and options. To help you get the most out of the software, you might want to take a minute and define a few key preferences. You can add and modify facts, determine the display of some windows, choose how common tasks are performed, add user information, change date formats, and even decide how Family Tree Maker handles data entry.

General Preferences

You can set some preferences that affect the interface and general workings of Family Tree Maker.

1. Click **Tools>Options**. Then click the **General** tab.

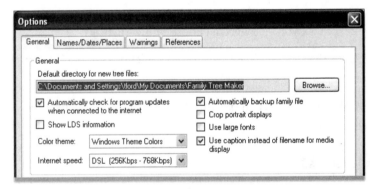

2. Change the General preferences as necessary:

   - **Default directory for new tree files.** Shows the default location where tree files are saved on your hard drive. If you want to change the default location, click **Browse** to choose where you want trees to be saved.

   - **Automatically check for program updates when connected to the Internet.** Click this checkbox if you want Family Tree Maker to automatically look for software updates when you're online. You will be alerted if an update exists.

- **Show LDS information.** Click this checkbox if you want LDS fields such as sealings and baptisms to be displayed.

- **Color theme.** Choose the color theme you want Family Tree Maker to use from the drop-down list. You can use default Ancestry colors (light green), the display colors you've chosen for your Windows operating system, or the classic blue Windows color.

- **Internet speed.** Choose the Internet connection you're using from the drop-down list.

- **Automatically back up family file.** Click this checkbox if you want Family Tree Maker to automatically create backups of your trees when you exit the program. If your original tree is ever lost or damaged, you can use the backup to restore your information. However, because the backup file takes up space on your hard drive, you may not want to use this option if hard drive space is limited.

- **Crop portrait displays.** If you have assigned a portrait to an individual, a thumbnail version of the photo appears in the pedigree view and editing panel. Click this checkbox if you want to resize thumbnail images so they fill the frame.

  Note: The actual images in your file will not be modified. Also, you cannot choose to resize individual thumbnails. This option resizes every thumbnail image in your file.

- **Use large fonts.** Click this checkbox to make the fonts in Family Tree Maker larger and more readable.

  Note: A larger font may help readability, but some labels may not display correctly and may be shortened.

- **Use caption instead of filename for media display.** Click this checkbox if you want to sort media items by the captions you have assigned them in Family Tree Maker. If you don't select this checkbox, media items will be sorted and displayed by filename.

- **PDF driver.** If you don't want to use the default PDF driver within Family Tree Maker, you can choose your own driver from this drop-down list.

Fastfields Preferences

Fastfields speed up data entry by automatically filling in repetitive data as you type. For example, if you type "San Jose, California, USA" into a location field, then go to another location field and begin to type "San," Family Tree Maker will recognize the similarity and suggest "San Jose, California, USA." By default, all Fastfields are selected, but you can turn off any that you'd like to.

1. Click **Tools**>**Options**. Then click the **General** tab.

2. In the "Use fastfields for" section, click the checkboxes for each type of field you want to turn off Fastfields for: names, places, sources, and/or descriptions.

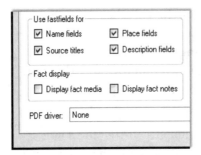

Fastfields

Fastfields is a special feature that allows you to save time by not having to enter the same information over and over again. Perhaps you noticed that as you begin typing a surname that Family Tree Maker automatically filled it in for you. This is because name fields, among others, are Fastfields.

Location Fastfields remember the names of any location you've entered into a tree. This means that when you move the cursor into a location field and start typing the name of a town that you've previously entered into Family Tree Maker, Fastfields automatically tries to fill it in for you. In addition, Family Tree Maker contains a database of more than 3 million place names, and as you type in a location, Family Tree Maker will suggest possible matches. Type the name of the town until Family Tree Maker suggests the right location; then use the keyboard arrows to highlight the location and press Enter to select it. You can also keep typing a name to override the Fastfields suggestion.

Online Searching Preferences

The Family Tree Maker Web Search feature can automatically search the databases at Ancestry.com for records and family trees that match individuals in your file. You can determine whether or not you want Family Tree Maker to search every time you connect to the Internet.

1. Click **Tools>Options**. Then click the **General** tab.

2. Change these online searching preferences as necessary:

    •   **Search online automatically.** Click this checkbox if you want Family Tree Maker to automatically search Ancestry.com for more information on individuals in your tree when your Internet connection is available.

        Family Tree Maker will conduct a behind-the-scenes search on each person and alert you when it has found relevant search results. You will see a green leaf next to an individual's name on the pedigree view when possible matches (hints) have been found. If you deselect this feature, you can still search online for your family members if you have an Internet connection by going to the Web Search workspace and entering your own website and search criteria.

    •   **Exclude Ancestry.com Family Trees from automatic search.** Click this checkbox if you don't want Ancestry.com Member Trees to be displayed in Ancestry hints.

    •   **Show Web Search help dialog.** Click this checkbox if you want to display a window that explains how to use the Web Merge when you begin an online search.

Spell Checking Preferences

You can determine how the spell check in Family Tree Maker should work, specifically what words it should ignore. The default setting is to ignore words in uppercase and to ignore HTML tags. Most likely you will want to leave the default setting for ignoring uppercase words; in family history, some individuals use capital letters for surnames to distinguish them from first and middle names.

> Note: You can use the dictionary to add words that you want the spell checker to ignore. You might want to add unusual family surnames or place names that will appear often in your tree.

Fact Display Preferences

The editing panel on the right side of the Person tab shows an individual's name and dates and information about the currently selected fact. Below this, you'll see a Sources tab. If you want, you can use the Fact display preferences to also display a Media tab and a Notes tab in the editing panel.

1. Click **Tools>Options**. Then click the **General** tab.

2. In the "Fast display" section, click the checkbox for each type of tab you want to display on the People tab's editing panel: Media tab and Notes tab.

Date Preferences

Family Tree Maker allows you to change the way dates are formatted. If you do not like the selections you've made, you can always reset your preferences by clicking the Use Defaults button.

1. Click **Tools**>**Options**. Then click the **Names/Dates/Places** tab.

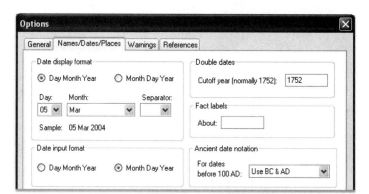

2. Change these date preferences as necessary:

   - **Date display format.** Choose how you want Family Tree Maker to display dates. Click **Day Month Year** if you want the day to appear before the month (e.g., 07 January 2011). By default, Family Tree Maker displays dates in this accepted genealogical date standard. Click **Month Day Year** if you want the month to appear before the day (January 07, 2011).

     Click the drop-down lists to choose different formats for the day, the month, and the date separator.

   - **Date input format.** Choose how you want Family Tree Maker to interpret dates you enter: day, month, year, or month, day, year. For example, if you enter "6/7/10" Family Tree Maker can read this as June 7th or July 6th.

   - **Double dates.** Change the year in this field to change the default double date cutoff year. If you do not want double dates to print, set the double date cutoff year to zero.

Note: Calendars used in Europe and the United States changed systems in 1752—moving from Julian to Gregorian. In the Julian system, the first day of the year was 25 March. In today's Gregorian system, 1 January is the first day of the year. Dates that fall between January and March of 1752 can be interpreted in two ways, and some genealogists prefer to show both dates. For example, February 22 could fall in the year 1750 according to the Gregorian calendar, so the date would be noted as 22 February 1750/51.

- **Fact labels.** To display a different abbreviation for the term "About" (meaning "Circa"), enter your preferred label.

    Note: If you change these labels, they will apply from this time forward. Dates that have already been entered using a different label will remain unchanged.

- **Ancient date notation.** Choose whether you want dates before 100 AD to be displayed with BC/AD or BCE/CE.

Name Preferences

Family Tree Maker lets you determine how names are displayed in the Index panel on the People workspace. You can include titles, alternative names, and married names for females. If you do not like the selections you've made, you can always reset your preferences by clicking the Use Defaults button.

1. Click **Tools>Options**. Then click the **Names/Dates/Places** tab.

2. Change these name preferences as necessary:

    - **Use AKA if available after middle name.** Click this checkbox to have names in Also Known As facts included with the preferred name (for example, Bobbitt, Mary Eliza "Mollie").

- **Use AKA if available as an additional entry.** Click this checkbox to have names in Also Known As facts appear as their own entries in the Index panel (for example, Hannah "Anna" Willis).

- **Use titles if available.** Click this checkbox to have titles in Title facts included with the preferred name (for example, Hait, Captain Samuel).

- **Use married names for females.** Click this checkbox to have women listed by their married (and maiden) names (for example, Hoyt, Maria Hitchcock).

Place Preferences

Family Tree Maker lets you determine whether place names entered in your tree are compared against the software's location database. If you do not like the selections you've made, you can always reset your preferences by clicking the Use Defaults button.

1. Click **Tools>Options**. Then click the **Names/Dates/Places** tab.

2. Change these place preferences as necessary:

- **Check place authority when entering place names.** Click this checkbox if you want Family Tree Maker to compare each place you enter against its database of locations. This option helps you keep your locations in standard formats and consistent throughout your tree.

- **Exclude selected country from resolved place names.** When you enter a place name, you usually include a country's name. However, if most events in your tree occur in the same country (for example, if most of your ancestors were born and died in England), you may not want to include a country's name in place fields and charts and reports. To keep a country's name from appearing, choose it from the drop-down list.

Warning and Alert Preferences

Family Tree Maker can automatically check your tree for errors and alert you if it detects a possible error, such as an illegal character or unusual dates.

1. Click **Tools**>**Options**. Then click the **Warnings** tab.

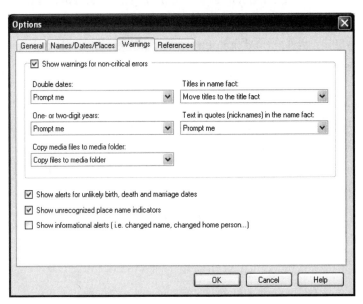

2. Change these warning preferences as necessary:

   • **Show alerts for unlikely birth, death, and marriage dates.** Click this checkbox if you want to be alerted when dates you enter don't seem accurate (for example, a death date that occurs earlier than a birth date).

   • **Show unrecognized place name indicators.** Click this checkbox if you want to be alerted when Family Tree Maker doesn't recognize a location you have entered.

     Note: This checkbox is grayed out if you have deselected the "Check place authority" option on the General tab.

   • **Show informational alerts.** Click this checkbox if you want to be alerted when you update your Family Tree Maker tree—for example, when you change the home person or update an individual's name.

The "Show warnings for non-critical errors" section lets you choose how you want Family Tree Maker to handle minor errors:

- **Double dates.** If Family Tree Maker detects double dates, you can choose to leave the dates as they are, use special formatting to show both dates, or be prompted for instructions.

- **Titles in name fact.** If Family Tree Maker detects titles such as Jr. or Sr. in a name field, you can choose to leave the title in the name field, move the title to the title field, or be prompted for instructions.

- **One- or two-digit years.** If Family Tree Maker detects years entered with one or two digits, you can choose to accept the date as it is, change the date to the most recent century, or be prompted for instructions.

- **Text in quotes.** If Family Tree Maker detects nicknames (indicated by quotes) in a name field, you can choose to leave the nickname in the name field, move the nickname to the nickname field, or be prompted for instructions.

- **Copy media files.** When you add a media file to your tree, you can choose whether or not to automatically copy the file to a Family Tree Maker media folder or be prompted for instructions.

Managing Facts

Facts are the essential building blocks of your tree, where you record the details about your family that are important to you. In order to capture the information you care about, you might want to create your own facts or change which fields appear for the predefined facts that come with Family Tree Maker.

Creating a Custom Fact

Although Family Tree Maker comes with a variety of default facts, you may want to create custom facts that work for your family tree. For example, if you are trying to track your ancestors by censuses, you may want to create a custom fact for each census year. Or, if you have many ancestors who served in the Korean War or other conflicts, you can create a fact for each war.

1. Click **Edit>Manage Facts**. The Manage Facts window opens.

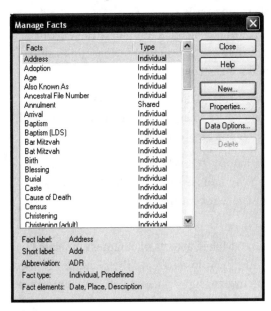

2. Click **New**. The Add Custom Fact window opens.

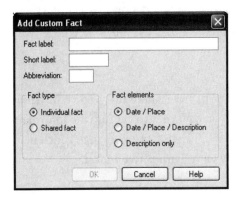

3. Change the fact as necessary:

    •   **Fact label.** Enter the name of the fact as it will appear on the
        Person tab.

    •   **Short label.** Enter a short name for the fact that will appear on
        the Family Tab editing panel; you can enter up to six characters.

- **Abbreviation.** Enter an abbreviation for the fact that will appear in reports; you can enter up to three characters.

- **Fact type.** Choose **Individual fact** if the fact applies to only one person, such as birth or death. Choose **Shared fact** if the fact applies to more than one individual, such as marriage.

- **Fact elements.** Choose the fields that you want to appear for the fact: Date and Place; Date, Place, and Description; or Description only.

4. Click **OK**.

Modifying a Predefined Fact

Family Tree Maker comes with many predefined facts. While you can't rename or delete these facts, you can choose which fields are included as part of the fact. For example, you can modify the Cause of Death fact so that only the Description field is included.

1. Click **Edit>Manage Facts**. The Manage Facts window opens.

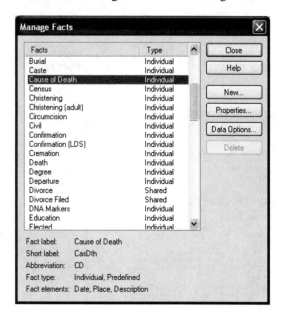

2. Click the predefined fact that you want to modify. Then click **Properties**. The Fact Properties window opens.

3. In **Fact elements**, choose which fields you want to appear for the fact. Then click **OK**.

Managing Historical Events

When you view an individual's timeline, or create a Timeline report, you have the option to include important historical events. Family Tree Maker comes with a set of default historical events that you can edit, delete, and add to. For example, you might want to add entries that are relevant to your family history, such as international events that caused your ancestors to immigrate, or natural disasters that affected your family.

1. Click **Edit>Manage Historical Events**. The Manage Historical Events window opens.

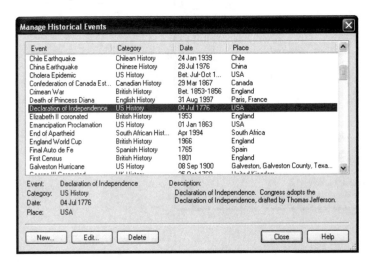

2. If you want to delete an event, click the entry and then click **Delete**.

3. To add an event click the **New** button. The Add/Edit Historical Event window opens.

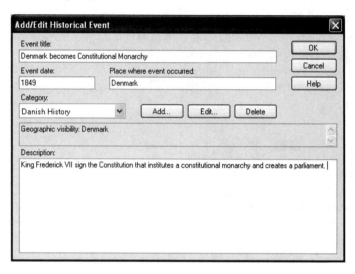

4. Change the historical event as necessary:

   • **Event title.** Enter a short title for the event.

   • **Event date.** Enter the date of the event.

   • **Place where event occurred.** Enter a location for the event.

   • **Category.** Choose a historical category from the drop-down list.

     Note: You can add your own categories or edit and delete the default categories.

   • **Description.** Enter a summary of the historical event.

5. Click **OK**.

Customizing the Family Tab Editing Panel

By default, these fields appear on the editing panel of the Family tab in the People workspace: Name, Sex, Birth Date, Birth Place, Death Date, Death Place, Marriage Date, and Marriage Place. If you often include burial information or christening dates for people in your tree, you can display these facts on the editing panel so you can enter the information more easily.

1. Go to the **Family** tab on the People workspace. The editing panel appears with its default fields.

2. Click **Customize View**. The Customize View window opens.

3. In the Individual facts section or the Shared facts section, click on the fact you'd like to add to the panel; then click the right arrow button to add the fact to the Selected facts sections.

4. To change the order in which the fields will display on the panel, click a fact in the Selected facts section and click the up or down arrows on the right side of the window.

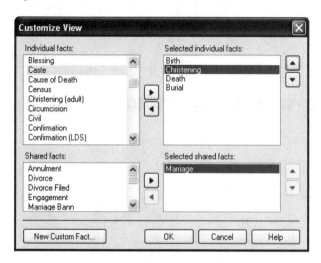

5. Click **OK**. The editing panel now includes the new fields.

Entering User Information

You can enter your personal information so that you will be identified as the person who created a tree. This information is then automatically added to your file if you contribute your tree to an online collection or export it and send it to another family member or researcher.

1. Click **Tools>User Information**. The User Information window opens.

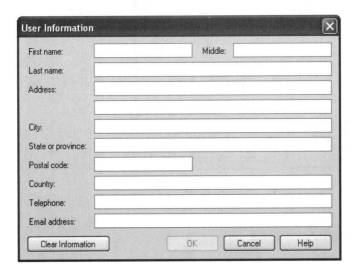

Note: If you are viewing another person's tree, the fields may already be completed. You can click the Clear Information button to clear the fields.

2. Enter your information and click **OK**.

Chapter Fourteen
Family Tree Problem Solver

No matter how organized you are or how carefully you enter data, eventually errors can creep into your tree. Whether you've linked a child to the wrong family or spelled your ancestor's name incorrectly, Family Tree Maker makes it easy to clean up your tree.

Resolving Relationship Issues

At some point in your research you may discover that a certain individual doesn't belong in your tree and you need to delete him or her. Or maybe you attached a child to the wrong family. Family Tree Maker makes it easy to change relationships between individuals when it's necessary.

Merging Duplicate Individuals

After months and years of gathering names and dates, eventually your family tree may become a bit disorderly. You might discover that the Flossie in your tree is actually the Florence you also have in your tree—not two distinct individuals. If you have two individuals you've entered in your tree who are the same person, you will want to merge them (instead of deleting one) so that you don't lose any information.

Family Tree Maker has a tool that can quickly assess your family tree and show you individuals who could possibly match each other.

Note: Before you merge individuals in your tree, you should make a backup of your tree. For instructions, see "Backing Up a File" on page 221.

Finding Duplicate Individuals

After adding a lot of new information or merging a family member's tree with yours, it's a good idea to check your tree for duplicate individuals.

1. Click **Edit>Find Duplicate People**. The Find Duplicate People window opens.

   In the Person 1 and Person 2 columns you'll see the individuals who might be duplicates. (You can click a column header if you want to sort the names alphabetically.) In the third column you'll see a match score— the higher the number the more likely the individuals are a match; a 1,000 means the individuals are almost exact matches.

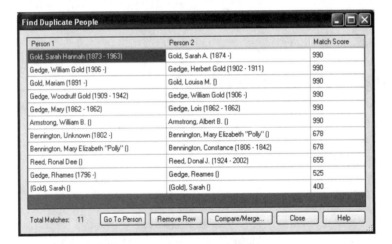

Person 1	Person 2	Match Score
Gold, Sarah Hannah (1873 - 1963)	Gold, Sarah A. (1874 -)	990
Gedge, William Gold (1906 -)	Gedge, Herbert Gold (1902 - 1911)	990
Gold, Mariam (1891 -)	Gold, Louisa M. ()	990
Gedge, Woodruff Gold (1909 - 1942)	Gedge, William Gold (1906 -)	990
Gedge, Mary (1862 - 1862)	Gedge, Lois (1862 - 1862)	990
Armstrong, William B. ()	Armstrong, Albert B. ()	990
Bennington, Unknown (1802 -)	Bennington, Mary Elizabeth "Polly" ()	678
Bennington, Mary Elizabeth "Polly" ()	Bennington, Constance (1806 - 1842)	678
Reed, Ronal Dee ()	Reed, Donal J. (1924 - 2002)	655
Gedge, Rhames (1796 -)	Gedge, Reames ()	525
(Gold), Sarah ()	(Gold), Sarah ()	400

Total Matches: 11   Go To Person   Remove Row   Compare/Merge...   Close   Help

2. If you want to merge a pair of individuals (or just compare the two), click their row in the window and click **Compare/Merge**. The Individual Merge window opens. For instructions on how to complete the merge, continue with step 5 in the next task, "Merging Individuals."

Merging Individuals

If you discover that two individuals in your tree are actually the same person, you can merge these two individuals together and retain all facts and dates associated with each person.

1. Go to the **Family** tab on the People workspace and select the appropriate individual.

2. Click **Person>Merge Two Specific Individuals**. The Index of Individuals window opens.

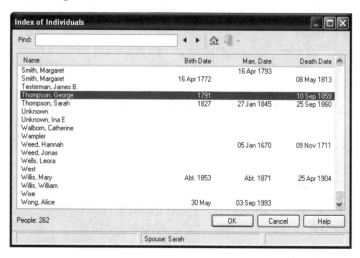

3. Click the name of the duplicate individual. You can use the scroll bar to move up and down the list, or type a name (last name first) in the **Find** field.

4. Click **OK**. The Individual Merge window opens.

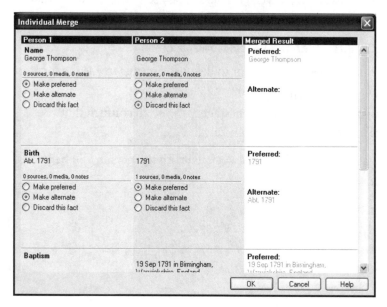

5. In the Person 1 and Person 2 columns, choose how you want each fact to be merged:

    -   **Make preferred.** Merge the information as the "preferred" fact for the individual.

    -   **Make alternate.** Merge the information as an alternate fact for the individual.

    -   Click **Discard this fact** to *not* merge the information into your tree. You may choose to discard some facts for a person, although it is usually a good idea to include all facts in case they turn out to be relevant. Click the **Keep sources** checkbox to merge the source information for the discarded fact.

    The Merged Result column shows all the facts that will exist for the merged individual.

6. Click **OK** to complete the merge.

Removing an Individual from Your Tree

If you find that you have mistakenly added an individual who isn't related to you, don't worry—Family Tree Maker makes it easy to delete the individual and his or her information from your tree.

1. Go to the **Family** tab on the People workspace.

2. Make sure the individual you want to delete from your tree is the focus of the pedigree view and the family group view.

3. Click **Person>Delete Person**. A message asks you to confirm that you want to delete the individual. Click **Yes**.

    All notes, tasks, and media links associated with the person will be permanently deleted.

    Note: Remember to use the Delete Person menu option whenever you want to remove someone permanently from your file. If you try to delete an individual by simply removing his or her name from the Name field, you won't actually delete the individual—or any of his or her facts or relationships. And if you delete a name and replace it with another, Family Tree Maker will mistakenly attach all the facts to the new individual, assuming that you have merely changed the name's spelling.

Removing a Marriage

As you continue your research you might find that you've entered a marriage for the wrong couple. You'll need to delete any marriage facts you've entered and also detach the individuals from each other.

1. Go to the **Family** tab on the People workspace and select the appropriate individual.

2. Click the **Person** tab. Then right-click the **Marriage** fact and choose **Delete Fact**. A message asks you if you want to delete this fact (and associated notes) from both individuals. Click **Yes**.

   Note: If you don't delete the Marriage fact, the individual will still be considered married but to an unknown person.

3. To detach the individual from the wrong spouse, click **Person>Attach/ Detach Person>Detach Selected Person**.

4. If necessary, choose which family you want to detach the individual from and click **OK**.

   Any children associated with the marriage will remain attached to the remaining spouse.

Detaching a Child from the Wrong Parents

If you have attached a child to the wrong parents, you can easily detach the child from the family without deleting the child from your family tree.

1. Go to the **Family** tab on the People workspace.

2. Make sure the family you want to detach a child from is the focus of the family group view. Then, click the child's name in the family group view.

3. Click **Person>Attach/Detach Person>Detach Selected Person**. The Detach window opens.

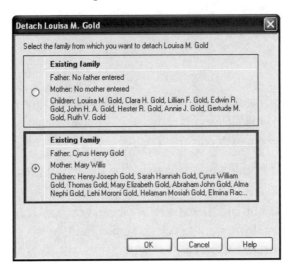

4. If necessary, choose which family you want to detach the individual from and click **OK**.

   The child is no longer connected to this family but remains in your tree. To access the individual at a later time, you'll need to locate him or her in the Index panel.

Attaching a Child to a Father and Mother

You might discover you have entered an individual and his or her parents into your tree, but you did not know they were related when you entered them. You can still link them together.

1. Go to the **Family** tab on the People workspace.

2. Make sure the individual you want to attach to his or her parents is the focus of the pedigree view and the family group view. If the child isn't in the direct line of the home person, you might need to select the individual in the Index panel.

3. Click **Person>Attach/Detach Person>Attach Mother/Father**. The Select the Mother/Father to Attach window opens.

4. Choose the father or mother from the list and click **OK**. If the father or mother has multiple spouses, you'll need to choose which family the child belongs to.

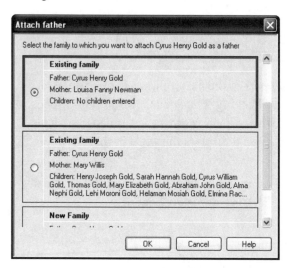

5. Choose the family to attach the individual to and click **OK**.

Fixing Data Entry Errors

It's easy to introduce data entry errors into your tree. Perhaps you transcribed a record too quickly or you imported incorrect notes from a family member's tree. Family Tree Maker has several tools that can help look for misspellings, inaccurate dates, and other data errors.

Global Spell Checker

The global spell checker lets you search for spelling errors in specific text fields in your file: the Description fields for all facts, the Caption and Description fields for media items, the Citation Detail and Citation Text fields for sources, and notes and to-do tasks.

1. Click **Tools>Global Spell Check**.

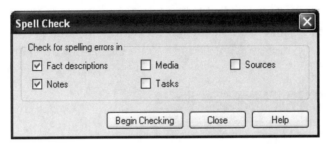

2. Click the checkbox for each part of the file you want Family Tree Maker to search. Then click **Begin Checking**. The Spell Check window opens and begins checking your tree for spelling errors. If Family Tree Maker detects a potential spelling error, it displays the word in the Not in dictionary field.

3. Replace or ignore the word using the spell check buttons. When a dialog box tells you that the spell check is complete, click **OK**.

Find and Replace Tool

You may have mistakenly spelled an individual's name wrong throughout your tree or perhaps you abbreviated a place name that you want to spell out now. You can use Find and Replace to quickly correct these mistakes—one-by-one or all at the same time.

1. Click **Edit>Find and Replace**. The Find and Replace window opens.

2. Enter the term you want to change in the **Find** field. Then enter the new term you want to use in the **Replace with** field.

3. Choose one or more of these options:

    - If you want to find words that match your search exactly (uppercase and lowercase), select the **Match case** checkbox.

    - If you want to find entire words that match your search, select the **Find whole words only** checkbox. (For example, a search for Will would not show results for William or Willton.)

    - If you want to search using wildcards, click the **Use wildcards** checkbox. Wildcards allow you to search for one or more "missing" characters. An asterisk (*) lets you search for multiple characters; a search for "Mas*" could find Massachusetts, Masonville, or Masterson. A question mark (?) lets you search for one character; a search for Su?an would find Susan and Suzan.

4. Choose which parts of your file you want Family Tree Maker to search in. If you're not sure where the information is, you might want to leave all the "Search in" checkboxes selected. Otherwise, choose the checkbox you want.

5. Click **Find**. The first result that matches your terms appears.

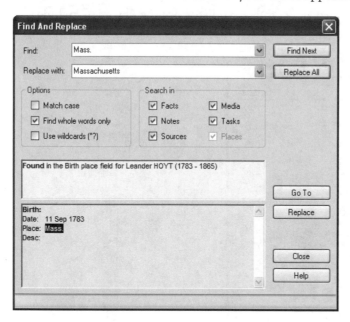

6. If you want to replace the current match, click **Replace**.

   Note: You can also replace all matching search results by clicking the Replace All button. Before you do so, you should back up your file because you cannot undo these changes.

7. To find the next matching term, click **Find Next**.

8. Continue searching and replacing terms, as necessary.

Running the Data Errors Report

Family Tree Maker can search your tree and identify potential errors it finds. For example, it can look for blank fields or date errors, such as an individual being born before his or her parents were born. It's a good idea to run this report periodically to make sure your tree is as error-free as possible.

1. Go to the **Collection** tab on the Publish workspace. In **Publication Types**, click **Person Reports**.

2. Double-click the **Data Errors Report** or click the report icon and then click the **Detail** tab.

3. To determine which errors the report lists, click the **Errors to include** button on the editing toolbar. The Errors to Include window opens.

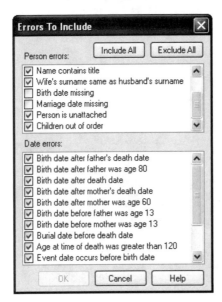

4. Click the checkboxes next to the errors you want Family Tree Maker to search your file for. Then click **OK**. The Data Errors Report opens.

Data Errors Report

Name	Birth Date	Potential Error
Anna Gedge	05 Sep 1865	The burial date occurred before his/her death.
Nathan Gedge	Abt. 1871	The birth date occurs after the death date. The birth date occurred after his/her mother was 60. The birth date occurred after his/her mother died. The birth date occurred after his/her father was 80. The birth date occurred more than one year after his/her father died.
Kate E. Kline	07 Nov 1857	The birth date occurs after the death date. Death date occurred before individual's birth date.
Mette Katrina Pedersen	22 Oct 1860	The individual has the same last name as her husband, Niels Pedersen. This individual's children sort order may be incorrect.
Mary Shanklin	1866	The birth date occurred more than one year after his/her father died.

5. If you want to change the error immediately, you can edit the information directly from the report by clicking on the individual's name.

Resolving Place Name Errors

Family Tree Maker contains a locations database of more than 3 million place names. When you import a GEDCOM or other genealogy file, or you manually enter a location name into your tree, Family Tree Maker automatically checks each place name against its database, looking for misspellings and missing data, such as missing counties. If any errors are found, or if the place does not match any locations in the Family Tree Maker database, a question mark icon appears next to the location's name in the Places workspace.

To keep your Family Tree Maker tree accurate *and* to make sure locations are recorded the same way every time they're entered, you'll want to examine each "unidentified" location and make any necessary changes. In some cases, you'll want to leave the name exactly as it is. For example, if the town or city no longer exists, or the county boundaries have changed over the years, you'll want to keep the location's name as you found it in the record. You can identify locations one at a time or as a group.

Resolving a Single Place Name

If you see a question mark icon next to a place name in your tree, you can try to identify the location in the Family Tree Maker database.

1. Click the **Places** button on the main toolbar. Click an unidentified location in the **Places** panel (one with a question mark icon next to it). In the panel on the right side of the window, you'll see the location's name and any people and events associated with it.

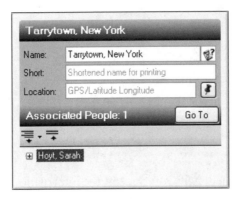

2. Click the question mark icon next to the place name in the editing panel. The Resolve Place Name window opens; the "Suggested place names" section lists the locations that most closely match the location in your tree.

3. If you find a location that matches the location in your tree, click its name in the "Suggested place names" section and then click **Replace**. If you do not find a location that matches the location in your tree, click **Ignore**.

   Whether you choose to accept or ignore the suggested name change, the location has been "identified," and the question mark next to the location's name will disappear.

Resolving Multiple Place Names

If you've imported a new tree or merged another person's tree into your own, you'll likely have many place names that don't match the other locations in your tree. Instead of updating each location one at a time, you can resolve many issues at one time.

1. Click **Tools>Resolve All Place Names**.

2. If you want to back up your file before you update your locations, click **Yes**. The Backup window opens. Change any options as necessary and click **OK**.

   The Resolve All Place Names window opens. Each location that Family Tree Maker doesn't recognize is listed—along with a suggested replacement location.

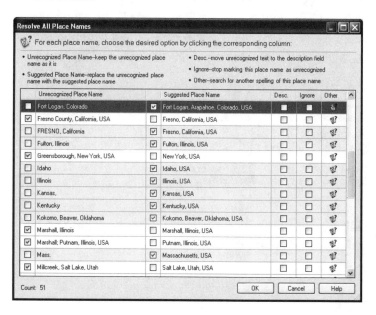

3. For each listed location, click the checkbox for the option you want to use:

   - **Unrecognized Place Name.** Click this checkbox if you want to keep the place name as it is currently listed.

   - **Suggested Place Name.** Click this checkbox if you want to change the current location's name to the suggested name.

   - **Desc.** Click this checkbox if you want Family Tree Maker to move the unrecognized place name from the Place field to the Description field.

   - **Ignore.** Click this checkbox if you want the unrecognized place name to be considered "recognized." The place name will not be considered an error in the future.

   - **Other.** If the suggested place name is incorrect, or you want to see other choices that might match the current place name, click **Other**. The Resolve Place Name window opens. Search for the location, or scroll through the suggested names. If you find the name you're looking for, click the name. Then click **Replace** to use the selected name.

4. When you've chosen an option for each location, click **OK**.

Finding Missing Media Items

If you move a media item on your computer, Family Tree Maker won't be able to open it, and you'll see a red link saying that the file cannot be found (fig. 14-1). Family Tree Maker has a tool that can relink all your missing media items at once.

Figure 14-1

A missing file on the Media workspace.

> Filename and location:
>
> File not found - Media0093.jpg
>
> C:\Documents and Settings\tlord\Desktop\Family Tree Maker\PedersenReed_2007-3 Media

1. Click the **Media** button on the main toolbar. Click **Media>Find Missing Media**. A list of unlinked images appears.

2. Click the checkboxes next to the items you want to look for or click **Select All** to find all broken media links.

3. Click **Search**.

   If Family Tree Maker is able to find the file, its current location is displayed in the Path column and a checkmark appears in the status column. If Family Tree Maker isn't able to find the file, it will be highlighted. You will need to click the item and search for it manually.

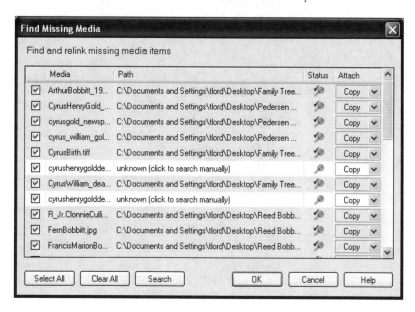

4. When you're finished, click **OK**.

Troubleshooting Computer Issues

Although we hope you never have problems while using Family Tree Maker, all computers and software have their own incompatibilities. This chapter covers a variety of difficulties you might encounter, such as installation problems. If you do need assistance, you may be able to locate the appropriate topic in this chapter and then fix the problem.

If you don't find an answer to your question, you can get help at <www.familytreemaker.com/support>. Click the "Knowledge Base" link. Enter your issue in the **Keyword Search** field and click **Search**.

Checking System Requirements

If you are having problems, you should make sure that your computer meets or exceeds the minimum requirements listed on page 4. Also, keep in mind that the more information you enter, the greater the amount of free hard drive space and available RAM you will need. If you plan to include many pictures, audio, or video files in your trees, you will need a substantial amount of hard drive space.

LEGAL DISCLAIMER
IMPORTANT—READ CAREFULLY BEFORE FOLLOWING TROUBLESHOOTING TIPS

FAMILY TREE MAKER HAS MADE EVERY EFFORT TO MAKE THE INFORMATION CONTAINED IN THIS GUIDE ACCURATE, COMPLETE, AND USEFUL. HOWEVER, INACCURACIES, ERRORS, AND OMISSIONS MAY OCCUR. ALL RECOMMENDATIONS, STATEMENTS, AND PROCEDURES ARE GIVEN WITHOUT WARRANTY OF ANY KIND. THE USER ASSUMES ALL RISKS ASSOCIATED WITH USE OF THIS GUIDE.

Installation Problems

If you are having difficulty installing Family Tree Maker on one computer, you should test the CD on another computer to verify that the disc is good. If the installation CD is damaged, contact customer support for assistance.

My system locks up during installation. (You may also see the message, "This program has performed an illegal operation and will be shut down.")
Close any programs you're using including shortcut toolbars and any antivirus programs. Then try reinstalling the software.

Nothing happens when I put the CD in the CD drive.
There may be fingerprints, scratches, or dust on your CD. Remove the CD from your CD-ROM drive and gently wipe it with a clean towel. Do not wipe in a circular motion around the CD; instead, wipe from the inside edge to the outside edge.

The Windows Autorun feature may be turned off. You'll need to start the installation program yourself. Make sure the CD is in the CD drive.

- **Windows XP.** Click the Windows **Start** button and select **Run.**

- **Windows 7 and Vista.** Click the Windows **Start** button and select **All Programs>Accessories>Run.**

In the **Open** field, type "d:setup". (The "d" in "d:setup" stands for drive D. If you are installing from a drive other than drive D, type that letter instead. For example, from drive E, type "e:setup".) Then click **OK.**

I get a message saying there isn't enough hard drive space to install the program.
You may be out of space on the drive where Windows is installed, the drive where you're attempting to save, or the drive where your temporary folder is located. To ensure that you have sufficient hard drive space, check the following:

- **Hard drive space available on the drive where Windows is installed.**
  You need to have at least 460MB of space available on the drive where

Windows is installed. In addition, Windows needs at least 150MB of free hard drive space to run properly after Family Tree Maker has been installed. You may encounter problems if you have less.

- **Hard drive space available on the drive where Family Tree Maker is saving your trees.** You generally need to have three times the size of your file available because of the way many Windows programs (including Family Tree Maker) save files. For example, if your file is 400,000 bytes, you actually need 1,200,000 bytes (1.2MB) available to save it.

- **Temporary hard drive space.** Windows maintains a temporary folder, usually C:\Windows\Temp, for temporary storage space. This folder can get very full over the months and should be cleaned out on a regular basis. To do this, first close all programs. Go to the Windows Temp folder and delete everything in it. To access the Temp folder, do one of these options: In Windows XP click the Windows **Start** button and select **Run**. In Windows 7 or Vista click the Windows **Start** button and select **All Programs>Accessories>Run**. Then, in the **Open** field, type "temp" and click **OK**. Windows opens the Temp folder. (Make sure the window's title bar says "Temp" before you delete any files.)

I get a message saying, "Cannot find d:setup."

The "d" in "d:setup" stands for drive D. If you are installing from a drive other than drive D, access the correct drive.

I get a message saying, "You must be logged on as an administrator." (Windows 7 and Vista)

In Windows 7 and Vista, access to common tasks and programs is managed by the User Account Control (UAC). If you are trying to access Family Tree Maker as a standard user (meaning without administrative privileges), you won't be able to open the program. You will need to run Family Tree Maker as an administrator. If you need instructions, go to the Family Tree Maker Knowledge Base; then enter "3779" in the search field and click **Search**.

How do I manually uninstall Family Tree Maker 2011?

If you have uninstalled and reinstalled the Family Tree Maker program and it still opens with the error message, "Program has encountered a problem and must close" (or similar message), you may need to manually remove Family Tree Maker. To troubleshoot this issue (and learn how to uninstall the program), go to the Family Tree Maker Knowledge Base; then enter "4848" in the search field and click **Search**.

File Importing Errors

I get an error message when I try to import a tree.

It is important to determine if the importing problem is specific to one single file or to several files. If you can import some files but not others, the file may be damaged. You may need to revert to a backup of your file. If you cannot import *any* files, create a new test file in Family Tree Maker and export it as a GEDCOM. Now try to import the test file. If it doesn't import, you'll need to uninstall and reinstall the software. For more information, go to the Family Tree Maker Knowledge Base; then enter "4400" or "4848" in the search field and click **Search**.

I am having trouble importing a large tree file. What can I do?

Family Tree Maker lets you import a tree using a low memory option. This process will write the file directly to your hard drive instead of using your computer's memory. It will take more time than the standard import but may allow you to import a file you normally wouldn't be able to. For instructions on using the low memory import, go to the Family Tree Maker Knowledge Base; then enter "5233" in the search field and click **Search**.

Web Search Problems

I get an error message when I start a Web Search that says, "You are not connected to the Internet or are behind a firewall."

This error occurs when your Internet connection is not active, or when something is blocking Family Tree Maker from using your Internet connection.

Make sure Internet access is enabled in Family Tree Maker. To do this, go to the **File** menu and select **Go Online**. (If the menu option "Go Offline" appears, Internet access is already enabled.)

Check your Internet connection. If you have a dial-up Internet connection, or you have disabled your broadband connection, establish your Internet connection before you open Family Tree Maker. Make sure you are able to get to other websites. If you are still unable to use the Web Search, you can troubleshoot this issue. Go to the Family Tree Maker Knowledge Base; then enter "2257" in the search field and click **Search**.

When I click on an Ancestry hint, the results are blank and I get a message saying that I have no unreviewed hints. How do I get rid of these empty hints?
These "phantom" hints usually mean that trees on Ancestry have been updated but the changes haven't been reindexed. You will continue to see these hints until the information is reindexed.

Performance Issues

Family Tree Maker is running slowly. What can I do?
If Family Tree Maker is running more slowly than expected, here are a few steps you can take to increase the software's performance.

- Make sure your computer meets or exceeds the minimum system requirements listed on page 4.

- Run the Compact File tool. Family Tree Maker's Compact File tool will re-index your file, remove unnecessary data, and optimize your tree's performance. (For instructions, see "Compressing a Tree File" on page 223.)

- Check your tree for duplicate individuals or sources. Merge them as necessary.

- Work offline. Consider temporarily disabling Internet access in Family Tree Maker. To do this, go to the **File** menu and choose **Go Offline**. If you don't want to disable Internet access, you might want to turn off Family Tree Maker's automatic Ancestry.com search feature. To do this go to the **Tools** menu and choose **Options**. In the window that appears, uncheck **Search online automatically when connected to the internet** and click **OK**.

- Disable Fastfields. Disabling Fastfields in large databases can also speed things up. To do this, go to the **Tools** menu and choose **Options**. In the window that opens, uncheck all checkboxes under the "Use fastfields for section" and click **OK**.

Program Unexpectedly Shuts Down

Family Tree Maker may shut down unexpectedly, and you may get an error message.

I get a message saying, "Family Tree Maker has encountered an error and needs to close" or "Family Tree Maker has stopped working."
These messages have been known to occur occasionally after Family Tree Maker has been uninstalled and then reinstalled or when a software patch has been installed to the software. Usually this message is caused by an old or corrupt Family Tree Maker configuration file. For instructions on deleting this file go to the Family Tree Maker Knowledge Base; then enter "5029" in the search field and click **Search**.

Family Tree Maker keeps crashing. What can I do?
All applications, no matter how stable, crash from time to time. However, if you are having problems with Family Tree Maker crashing frequently you may want to follow the steps outlined below to help resolve this issue. You should create a backup of your file before continuing with any of these processes.

- Confirm that your Windows software is up-to-date. If you don't know how to do this, please refer to the appropriate Microsoft help articles:

  For Windows XP go to <http://www.microsoft.com/windows/downloads/windowsupdate/learn/windowsxp.mspx>.

  For Vista go to <http://www.microsoft.com/windows/downloads/windowsupdate/learn/windowsvista.mspx>.

  For Windows 7 go to <http://windows.microsoft.com/en-us/windows7/Install-Windows-updates>.

- Periodically, Family Tree Maker releases updates that fix various software bugs and issues. Make sure that the Family Tree Maker software is up-to-date by going to the **Help** menu and choosing **Check for Update**. A message alerts you if you need to update the software.

If Family Tree Maker continues to crash, you can find more information on this issue on the Family Tree Maker Knowledge Base. For Windows XP users, enter "4442" in the search field and click **Search**; for Vista users, enter "5157"; and for Windows 7 users, enter "5158".

Printing Problems

Many printing problems are related to the specific printer you are using. Before you begin, make sure your printer is hooked up correctly, is turned on, and is connected to the computer. Also, make sure you're familiar with any documentation that came with your printer. If you don't find your issue in the topics below, you may want to contact technical support for the printer's manufacturer.

I am unable to print in Family Tree Maker.

Try to print an image or document from another software program. This will verify whether or not the printer is functioning properly. If you can print an image using another program, the issue may be a conflict with Family Tree Maker.

The most common cause of printing issues involves conflicts between the program and printer driver, which acts as a translator between the printer and the application. Verify that the driver for your printer is up-to-date. Contact the printer manufacturer for the latest driver for the printer in use. Most manufacturers offer these updated drivers as free downloads from their websites.

Your computer may be running low on memory or resources. Family Tree Maker requires that you have at least 1GB of physical memory to run. If you don't have enough memory, Family Tree Maker might run slowly at times and might take a long time to perform certain tasks like printing, especially if you have a large tree. Try closing other programs to make more memory available. If the performance is still sluggish, you might want to consider adding more memory to your system.

Why is Family Tree Maker printing slowly?

Printing from Windows, especially when printing graphics, can be slow. If you want to print faster, you can try printing images at a lower quality. Be aware that the output won't look as nice.

The Windows spool settings may be slowing the printing down. To disable these features, see your Microsoft Windows user's guide. You may also need to consult the documentation that came with your printer.

My photos are not printing clearly.

Try selecting a different image format when you import the graphic file. Family Tree Maker accepts a variety of common file formats.

The image may have been poor quality to begin with. If possible, get a better quality image.

Family Tree Maker crashes when I print charts and reports.

Verify that the driver for your printer is up-to-date. Contact the printer manufacturer for the latest driver for the printer in use. Most manufacturers offer these updated drivers as free downloads from their websites.

PDF Problems

I am unable to save a chart as a PDF.

If you encounter problems using the PDF functions when you're saving reports and trees as PDFs, you need to designate yourself as an administrator on your computer. If you need instructions, go to the Family Tree Maker Knowledge Base; then enter "3779" in the search field and click **Search**.

Also, be aware that PDFs are limited to 200 inches by 200 inches. If your chart is larger than this, the contents will be truncated.

Software Updates

How can I make sure I have the latest software updates?

Periodically, Family Tree Maker releases updates that fix various software bugs and issues. Make sure that the Family Tree Maker software is up-to-date by going to the **Help** menu and choosing **Check for Update**. A message alerts you if you need to update the software.

In Windows 7 and Vista, you will need to run Family Tree Maker as an administrator in order to check for updates. If you need instructions, go to the Family Tree Maker Knowledge Base; then enter "3779" in the search field and click **Search**.

Display Problems

Family Tree Maker windows will not display correctly. Buttons and fields overlap each other and are difficult to read. How can I fix this?

Display problems can occur if you have changed the default display font size. You will need to change your Windows font size back to the default, or you can drag a window to enlarge it. For more information on this issue, go to the Family Tree Maker Knowledge Base; then enter "2937" in the search field and click **Search**.

Registration Issues

I am having a problem registering the software.

Your computer may not be connected to the Internet. Make sure that you are able to access and log in to Ancestry.com using a normal Web browser (Internet Explorer, etc.). If you are unable to access the website you'll need to fix your Internet connection before trying to register.

———————

Make sure Internet access is enabled in Family Tree Maker. To do this, go to the **File** menu and select **Go Online**. (If the menu option "Go Offline" appears, Internet access is already enabled.)

———————

Your firewall settings or security software may be preventing Family Tree Maker from starting the registration process. You may need to add FTM.exe as an exception to your security software or firewall. For information about changing firewall settings, contact your security software manufacturer directly.

———————

Make sure that your computer's date and time are correctly set to your time zone. If you need help, check your computer's Help or user's manual.

Damaged or Corrupt Files

I don't have a backup of my tree and my file isn't working. Is there anything I can do?

Files can be damaged by viruses, a merging of corrupt data, the improper shut down of Family Tree Maker, and more. If you don't have a backup of your tree, you can try to fix the damage to your current file. For help, go to the Family Tree Maker Knowledge Base; then enter "5146" in the search field and click **Search**.

Glossary

ancestor A person you descend from—parents, grandparents, great-grandparents, etc.

Ancestry Member Tree A family tree you have created on or uploaded to Ancestry.com.

browser See Web browser.

click The action of pressing and releasing a mouse button. Usually, when a program instructs you to click an item, it is referring to the left side of the mouse. A program may specify "left-click" or "right-click." You can also double-click by pressing and releasing the mouse button twice in rapid succession.

descendant A person who descends from you—your children, grandchildren, great-grandchildren, etc.

descendant chart A chart that lists an individual and his or her descendants.

editing panel A section of a workspace that lets you easily edit and view information for a specific individual or item you have entered in Family Tree Maker.

export To transfer data from one computer to another or from one computer program to another.

family group sheet A form that displays information about a single, complete family unit—father, mother, and children.

family group view Shows a single family unit—parents and their children—in Family Tree Maker.

Fastfields Family Tree Maker remembers the names of the locations and people you have typed in so that when you begin to type a place in a new location field or a surname in a name field, Family Tree Maker shows you possible matches based on the letters you have typed up to that point.

GEDCOM GEnealogical Data COMmunication. A standard designed by the Family History Department of The Church of Jesus Christ of Latter-day Saints for transferring data between different genealogy software packages.

genealogy report A narrative-style report that details a family through one or more generations and includes basic facts about each member in addition to biographical information that was entered through Family Tree Maker.

generation The period of time between the birth of one group of individuals and the next—usually twenty-five to thirty-three years.

given name The first name (and middle name) given to a child at birth or at his or her baptism. Also known as a Christian name.

home or primary person The main individual in your tree.

homepage The main page of a website.

icon A small graphic picture or symbol that represents a program, file, or folder on your computer. Double-clicking an icon with a mouse generally causes the program to run, the folder to open, or the file to be displayed.

import To bring a file into a program that was created using another program.

maternal ancestor An ancestor on the mother's side of the family.

media item Photographs, scanned documents, audio files, or videos that you can add to a tree.

paternal ancestor An ancestor on the father's side of the family.

PDF Portable Document Format. A file format (.PDF) that retains printer formatting so that when it is opened it looks as it would on the printed page. It requires Adobe Reader to view.

pedigree chart A chart that shows the direct ancestors of an individual. Also known as an ancestor tree.

pedigree view The pedigree tree on the People workspace that lets you see multiple generations of a family and navigate to other members of your family tree.

preferred A term Family Tree Maker uses in reference to parents, spouses, or duplicate events indicating that you want to see the preferred selection first or have it displayed in trees and reports.

root person The individual who is currently the focus of the workspace or charts or reports.

siblings Children of the same parents.

Soundex A system that assigns a code to a surname based on how it sounds rather than how it is spelled.

source   The record, such as a book, an e-mail message, or an interview, from which specific information was obtained.

spouse   The person to whom another person is married.

surname   The family name or last name of an individual.

timeline   A visual representation of events over time.

tree   The Family Tree Maker name for the database that contains the information about your lineage, e.g., you could create a tree for the Smith family or Jones family.

Web browser   The software that lets you access pages on the Web. The browser reads the HTML code and converts it to the pictures, colors, menu options, and overall design that you view on your monitor.

Web clipping   The ability to "clip" text or images from a Web page and merge it into a Family Tree Maker file.

Web Dashboard   A feature on the Plan workspace that lets you view your Ancestry.com account information.

Web Merge   The ability in Family Tree Maker to take search results you've found online and merge them into your tree.

Web Search   A Family Tree Maker function that automatically searches Ancestry.com for records containing information about your ancestors.

Web page or website   A location on the Web maintained by a single individual, company, or entity that provides information, graphics, and other items.

workspace   A major grouping of Family Tree Maker features. Each workspace can be accessed from the main toolbar.

Index

W

About the Author

Tana L. Pedersen

Tana has been writing and editing in the technology industry for almost fifteen years. She has earned several awards for her writing, including the Distinguished Technical Communication award from the Society for Technical Communication. Tana is author of five editions of *The Official Guide to Family Tree Maker* and co-author of *The Official Guide to RootsWeb.com*.

Photo by Braden Lord